Everyone Versus Everyone

Story by Arthur Jay
Cover art and design by Dave Estes

ISBN 978-0692472972

This book is dedicated to M, M,

and everyone else.

Table of Contents

I

There's Going to Be a Trial

The alarm clock buzzed at 6AM, Monday morning. *Bzzz BZzz BZZzZZ.* Arthur Jay was lying in bed awake, after a sleepless night. The sun was just peeking over the rooftops in Arthur's neighborhood, glistening off the chimney caps, and the birds were chirping outside his bedroom window. *Chirp chirp. Time to get up Arthur Jay. Chirp chirp. Time to get up.*

Arthur yawned and stretched his arms over head. *All right already,* Arthur said to himself. *Time to get moving. Today's the big day.* Today was the day of the trial.

Arthur was ready for this day to come and go. The last few weeks had been tough. The media attention was overwhelming. Paparazzi shoved cameras and recorders in his face, everywhere he went. He couldn't buy groceries or pump gas without someone asking for a comment. Everyone wanted to know how he would testify. But his lawyer, Otto Griebel, had trained him well. *No Comment*, he'd say. *No comment.*

This morning, the stage fright was mounting. Visions of himself, stumbling or stuttering on the stand, floated past his mind. No less than the fate of America rested in part on his shoulders, and the whole world would be watching live. *You better not screw this up,* he told himself. As it always does on big days, doubt was knocking on the mind's door, but Arthur Jay wouldn't tolerate it. *Head up my man. Carry on. A man's got a job to do, and he's gotta do it.* So Arthur Jay pushed his blanket aside, stood up, and farted.

Standing in his bedroom, Arthur could see out the hallway window. News vans were parked on both sides of the street. On the sidewalks, cameramen unpacked their bags and linesmen ran cables in between a sea of people. Interviewers mingled amongst the crowd with microphones in hand, checking the pulse of the revelers and curiosity seekers who had gathered to get a first hand glimpse of Arthur Jay, one of the chosen six who would testify that day on behalf of the Plaintiff.

The *chopchopchop* of a helicopter echoed overhead. Policemen paced along the edge of Arthur's front lawn, standing proud in their navy blue uniforms. Up and down the barricaded street, policemen and spectators speculated on the substance and outcome of the trial, kidding about their plans for the money. To be fair, Arthur himself was thinking about the money, and what he was going to do with it. *Goddamn it.* But Arthur didn't like those thoughts. *Focus, my man,* he told himself. *It's not about the money.* And it really wasn't. At least at first. Arthur had signed up for this trial under completely different illusions, thinking that his testimony might matter, and that his words would make a difference. Now, on the big day, small inklings of doubt nibbled at the edge of his conscience. Arthur wondered if the trial might actually be a mistake. But there was no turning back. So Arthur took a deep breath, stepped out of his bedroom and got on with the morning.

A shower, shave, a cup of coffee, a bowl of cereal and a rinse of the hands later, Arthur Jay was standing in front of the mirror in his socks and underwear, holding up shirt and tie combos. Having settled on a yellow shirt and blue tie, Arthur put on his best pair of gray trousers. They were stained where he dropped a chicken wing, a week earlier, but a jacket would cover that. So Arthur pulled his favorite brown sports coat out of the closet and slipped it on. *Like a million bucks*, he thought as he adjusted himself in the mirror. Then without reason for delay, Arthur grabbed his keys, stepped out the front door and into the arms of destiny.

Immediately, flashbulbs went off. The police couldn't keep the media back. Like a pack of vultures they rushed at Arthur. "Mr. Jay, Mr. Jay. How are you feeling? Are you nervous? How will you testify? What are your thoughts?" A dozen cameramen and journalists crammed to hear Arthur's response. Arthur said nothing. Two officers with burly arms reached past the microphones to grab Arthur by the collar and tug him free of the pushing, elbowing, mass of media. The police rushed him to a waiting black town car where a chauffeur in a dark cap helped him into the back seat. Then, safe behind a locked door, Arthur rolled down the window and smiled at the cameras. He gave a thumbs-up and shouted. "Today's going to be a great day for America! Justice is in the air!" He rolled up the window and the car took off.

II

To the Courthouse

The ride from Arthur's cul-de-sac to the courthouse downtown was just long enough for Arthur to collect his breath and settle his thoughts before the long day. Arthur looked out the car window and dreamt back to the day six months ago when he sacrificed a whole Saturday to sign up for the trial. Under clear blue skies, Arthur spent a morning standing in line for the chance to speak for the Plaintiff in Otto's initial lawsuit, Springfield versus Springfield. It was a gimmick to be sure, but the radio ad promised free coffee and the chance to make a difference. Arthur stood in line with almost one hundred other early applicants for four hours, drinking coffee and chatting before he was called before Otto for an interview.

At first, applicants like Arthur Jay were in it just to make a political statement and do something different for a change. Attorney Otto Griebel was only interested in getting some publicity for his struggling practice. The morning after Arthur's interview, Arthur spotted himself in the local newspaper in the background of a black and white photo, stuffing a donut in his mouth. There he was with powdered sugar all over his black shirt, right next to a small squib about the speculative trial. Arthur was surprised when Otto called him back a week later to ask him to testify. "Of course I'll testify," Arthur replied.

Unbeknownst to Arthur, the story was spreading quickly. Within days of the phone call, an article appeared in the Chicago Tribune. The next day, USA Today, CNN, and the BBC picked up the story. Arthur, still oblivious, was shocked to see Otto

Griebel one night on his television set, speaking about the trial on an evening news show. Stone-faced, Otto addressed his fellow Americans in primetime.

"Good citizens of America. The proof is all around us. Democracy has failed. The promises of our forefathers were no more than whispers in the night. Life, liberty and the pursuit of happiness were mere sweet nothings, designed to butter us up. Look past the glitz and the glamor of your television sets and ask yourselves what's really going on. Are we really free, or just slaves to the illusion of the American Dream? Who here, doesn't expect more from this life? What ever happened to the honor of an honest day's work? Where did the time go, when values weighed more than gold? When did we abandon rock and roll for the corporate consistency of popular music? How many of us have traded our wild spirit for the cold comfort of a cubicle?

"Ladies and gentlemen, when did celebrity become the talent and not talent the celebrity? When did inequality become acceptable? When did we let medicine become big business or open up our prisons to investors? Who decided that profits trump trees? Why is politics a popularity contest, and not a means to a better world?

"Fellow Americans, look around you. Democracy is dead. Society isn't what it used to be, and the only way to justice is through the courts. So join me. Join us. Join our lawsuit. Everyone join everyone against everyone, in the class action lawsuit of Everyone versus Everyone, and let's settle this once and for all. For you. For me. For the promise of a better tomorrow."

Within twenty-four hours, the story of the trial went viral. Otto received emails and phone calls in droves. He had to upgrade his internet service and hire a secretary. In no time, the whole country was caught up in the mania. The first to sign on with the Plaintiff sensed little risk but great reward if they won. Eventually, even the skeptics joined in, for fear of being left behind. Besides, all they had to do was sign on the dotted line, cross their fingers, and pray for the money. The hysteria didn't break until each and every red-blooded American of voting age, from coast to coast and sea to shining sea, had officially signed on as Plaintiff. Thus was born the class action lawsuit of Everyone versus Everyone. For the sake of America, freedom and democracy, everyone was suing everyone.

Now that the day of the trial was here, Arthur Jay wasn't quite sure which side he was on. If everyone was suing everyone, and everyone was guilty, did that make him guilty, and if he was guilty, who was going to pay for this thing anyway?

The car started to slow. The driver put on his blinker and pulled into the exit lane. Arthur sat up. They were almost at the courthouse. As the car pulled up to a stoplight, Arthur could see the crowds in the distance. They stretched for a mile down Main Street toward the courthouse, and they got thicker as the car drew nearer. Thousands of gawkers of every color, creed and religion, stood six people deep on the sidewalks. The car came to a stop outside the courthouse. The chauffeur came around to open the door. As Arthur stepped out of the car, a whiff of deep fried falafel floated past his nose.

Across the street, a hipster with tattooed arms was yelling from a truck, "Falafel for a dollar, everyone eats for a buck!" Next to the truck an Asian man was selling t-shirts that read, "I sued everyone, and all I got was this lousy t-shirt." Next to him, a fat kid sipped a Big Gulp while his mother posed for a photo with a stranger in a cowboy hat. Revelers rejoiced up and down the street. College kids shot-gunned beers. Hippies rolled their own. Elderly with walkers sipped from flasks and told-you-so'd, and throughout the crowd, the media flittered, filming and recording everything. Somewhere a child let go of a red balloon. It floated up and over the stone facades of Main Street and into the clear blue sky.

"Arthur, Arthur," Otto called, "Good to see you, my man. Come on over!" Otto was standing with the five others who would testify. Arthur felt he had seen their faces before, that Saturday six months ago perhaps. Before him were Tyrone Jenkins, a black man dressed all in black, in baggy pants, a blousy shirt and a silk tie; PhD. Gustavo Jeremiah, an olive-skinned, middle aged man of medium height in green khaki pants and a gray sweater with longish black hair that fell thinly over his spectacles; Congresswoman May Farleigh, a vibrant brunette with tanned radiant skin in a well fitted navy blue pant suit, an American flag pinned to her lapel; twenty four year old Jackie Lim, a pretty girl of tanned skin, who could have fit in anywhere from Miami to Tokyo, and was provocatively dressed in black with a solitary streak of red in her jet black hair; and finally great Greta Gernhart, a large, gray-haired white women of mid-western roots in a purple flower print muumuu. Greta's arm fat jiggled as she waved to Arthur. Arthur was the last of the Plaintiffs to arrive. Otto stuck out his hand to greet him. "Arthur, my man, I'm glad you made it. Now that we're all here, I'd like to finally introduce you to the other Plaintiffs. Arthur, please meet Tyrone Jenkins, Greta Gernhart, Jackie Lim, former Congresswoman May Farleigh, and environmentalist Gustavo Jeremiah."

Gustavo nodded to Arthur. "You can call me Gus."

"Nice to meet you, Gus. Nice to meet you all," Arthur replied. Then Otto addressed the group, "Today's the big day folks. We've prepared plenty. There's not much more to say other than relax, take it easy. You'll be sitting for a long time, listening and observing. Don't drink too much water. There won't be many breaks. Sit up straight, smile at the cameras, and everything will go fine. When it's your turn to testify, just remember to breathe. With all that said, now that we're all here, let's head into the courthouse."

One by one, in single file, the group climbed the steep stone steps of the court. At the top of the stairs, between massive granite pillars they paused to turn around. The seven of them took one last look at the world, before everything might change forever. From up high, Arthur could make out just how far the crowds went. It was like a rock concert out there. Sweaty masses mingled in the bright sun, spending their change on funnel cakes, stick-on tattoos, carnival rides and cotton candy. Somewhere in the distance, on a big bare stage, an Elvis impersonator gave a rousing rendition of *Hound Dog* that could be heard all the way down, deep underground, in the cells under the courthouse, where optimistic criminals – Plaintiffs as well – counted the hours to the moment they might win their freedom. "Today's the big day, folks," Otto declared, "Today's the day we change the world." At that moment, a gust of wind blew down Main Street, rustling the leaves of the mighty oaks along the way. The breeze swept through Otto's magnificent brown hair and blew a chill up the back of Arthur's neck. The seven of them walked into the courthouse.

III

The Scene in the Courtroom

It was just eight in the morning, but the courtroom was already packed to capacity. The walls felt like they were falling in. Otto led the group down the center aisle toward the front row of the court benches. Arthur trailed behind Tyrone. He looked around as they walked to their seats.

At the back of the room, there were a dozen rows for the public. Tickets for seats in the public area had been drawn randomly from social security numbers, giving every American an equal chance to participate live. The crowd made up a rather representative cross section of society. Even ranch hand Miguel Sanchez, an illegal alien from south of the Rio Grande was able to sneak in past security. Around him, school teachers, janitors, retailers and engineers; bankers, tailors, athletes and artists; rich, poor, young and old; all races, genders and creeds; straight and gay, dumb and smart; people of every persuasion were represented in one way or another. There were neat professionals in business suits, paraplegics in wheel chairs, wild bearded hipsters in jeans, tattooed bikers and dainty housewives. There was a blind man with a cane, and a deaf man with an interpreter. Somewhere in the middle of the crowd, a man of Caribbean descent beat a small white drum with his strong dark hands while a loud Texan cheered for his team, shirtless, like a hooligan at a football match. *Let's go Everyone, Let's go,* chanted the Texan, while the Caribbean man *drum, drum, drumdrumdrum'd.*

Streamers of red, white and blue hung across the ceiling. The crest of the bald eagle over the judge's bench was covered in blue confetti. The bailiff, African-American Captain Anton Brown of the State

Police, stood stoically at the front of the room between an American flag and the media booth, dressed all in khaki with a black belt and a holstered pistol.

Anton looked annoyed. *They better not make me use this thing,* he thought as he glanced at the cameras. The media were acting the fools. The square media booth barely fit four on a good day. Today the booth was bursting at the seams with reporters and cameras from Fox News, CNN, Telemundo, Al Jazeera, the Associated Press and the BBC. Several local reporters were squeezed in between with note pads and tape recorders. Everyone was jostling for position, elbowing and knocking one another's equipment. CNN had a hand in the BBC's face. France24 stepped on Al Jazeera's foot. The CNN microphone smacked the local press on the visor, who dropped his notepad and bent to pick it up. He smacked his head on the BBC's chin while standing up and then bumped the Associated Press with his bottom. There was a great deal of cursing. Only Fox News was enjoying himself, having been shoved forcefully into the rear end of

Miss Telemundo, who now glared at him over her shoulder.

Across the courtroom, the Jury sat quietly, ignorant of the cause for the chaos around them. If any argument might have been made to delay this trial on technical grounds, it would have been that this jury was not a jury of everyone's peers. These eight jurors could not be everyone's peers, because everyone's peers were already signed up with the Plaintiff. These eight jurors were the only eight Americans who hadn't heard of the case and hadn't had a chance to sign up themselves. In fact, the trial would have started earlier except that they were waiting for the last juror, juror number one, to wake up from a coma.

Dear widowed Ruth was a sweet old lady, 82 years of age. Born and raised in Jamaica, Ruth came to America at the age of 18 to work in the tobacco fields. She fell in love with a man from Kingston, raised two lovely boys and three sweet grandkids. She went to church every Sunday, rain or shine. She prayed night and day. She was an avid reader and could quote a great deal of the Bible.

Eight months earlier, on a Saturday, immediately preceding her coma, Ruth fell off of a footstool while trying to kill a spider in her bathroom. In the process of falling, she knocked the bathroom door shut and landed on the can of Raid that she was using to kill the spider. So it went, the bottle discharged completely and the toxic gas knocked her out cold. When she didn't show up for church the next morning, her good friend Anne became suspicious and came to the house to inquire. A good Christian never locks her door, so when Ruth didn't come to the bell, Anne went right in and found her on the bathroom floor. The doctors thought she might not make it, but over eight months her signs never worsened, and then miraculously just twenty-four hours earlier, Ruth woke up. At 6:15 a.m. that morning, Ruth was released from the hospital. The doctor's might not have released her so soon, had they not been so eager to see this trial get underway.

Behind Ruth were three survivalists, middle-aged friends, who were discovered off the grid in the vast wilderness of Yellowstone National Park. The three men survived in the wilderness from the sweat of their brow, the skill of their hands and the speed of their feet. In the summer months they picked berries and set traps. In the winter they burned wood. All year long they fished. Their home was constructed of fallen logs, patched with mud and thatch, but it had a roof and it kept them safe. Upon their discovery, the air force sent in a helicopter to retrieve them and keep them under quarantine, lest they learn of the trial and form an opinion during transit. Even the Generals had skin in this game.

Jurors five and six were two smooth scalped, crimson-robed Buddhist monks, discovered meditating silently at a remote monastery in the Idaho badlands. The alternates, jurors seven and eight, had one body but two personalities. Marla and Sharla were pony-tailed Siamese twins of a feral persuasion, borrowed from the circus.

Arthur looked around and took it all in. He shook his head skeptically. He sat down at the end of the bench, next to Tyrone. Down the line, Greta, Jackie, Gus and Congresswoman Farleigh, sat in the order in which they would testify. Otto was seated just right of center in the middle of the courtroom at an oak table. Across the court to his left, the Public Defender sat alone at an identical oak table. Behind the Public Defender, the row for the Defendants was empty, except for three members of the Public who were let in at the last minute; a one-eyed man with a parrot on his shoulder, and two beautiful buxom blonde bombshells in short black dresses with tanned legs, strong calves and stunning black heels.

There was a knock from a door at the front of the courtroom behind Bailiff Anton Brown. Anton spoke, "All rise. The Honorable Judge Bacchus." Stenographer, Mary-Jane Reefer, a prim brunette in a gray skirt and white blouse began to type. The door behind Anton opened and Judge Bacchus stepped into the room. His black robes fluttered majestically with the winds of fate. He strode up the steps to his perch up high. Then firmly in his seat, under the confetti-strewn crest of the bald eagle, Judge Bacchus swung his gavel three times and declared, "Court is in session."

IV

Opening Remarks

Judge Maxwell Bacchus made an imposing figure, sitting up high on the bench. Underneath the eagle's confetti covered crest, his long wavy gray hair flowed neatly into his black robes. From the back of the courtroom, and on screens around the world, Judge Bacchus radiated an aura of authority. But Judge Bacchus couldn't stop himself from smiling and thinking, *a first row ticket to the fight of the century*. Inside, he was giddy, having already been paid handsomely and equally from both sides so that he would be biased in neither way. All he had to do was sit back and watch it all unfold.

With the utmost neutrality, Judge Bacchus swung his gavel and assumed a serious face. "Ladies and gentlemen, please be seated." The crowd settled in. Judge Bacchus continued, "Welcome to United States Central District Court. Today we'll hear the class action lawsuit of Everyone versus Everyone. Over the course of these proceedings, we will hear from the Plaintiff, who alleges that everyone is responsible for society's sordid state of affairs. Representing the Plaintiff will be Attorney Otto Griebel.

"On the other hand, the Defense will argue that it is not everyone who is guilty. Since everyone has signed up on behalf of the Plaintiff, and everyone is punch drunk insane over this trial, the court has assigned a Public Defender on everyone's behalf." Someone in the crowd booed. Over at the Defense's table, a dawdling, dumpy Public Defender looked up from his newspaper. He smiled sheepishly at the jury, and then nodded at the cameras.

"It will be up to the jury," Judge Bacchus continued, "to decide whether or not everyone is guilty; whether or not, through gross negligence or selfish participation in society – or lack thereof – everyone has directly or indirectly contributed to the poor state of society and everyone's general suffering. In order to right this wrong and rebalance the scales of justice, the Plaintiff is seeking sixteen trillion dollars in damages."

At the sound of *sixteen trillion dollars*, the courtroom stirred to life. Cameras flashed in the media booth. Captain Anton Brown rolled his eyes. The Caribbean man let out a little drum. *Ratatata tata tat ratatata tata tat.* The Texan made a tiny holler, trying oh-so-hard to restrain himself before the authority of God and the District Court. Over in the jury box, Ruth wrinkled her nose and scrunched her eyes. She clutched at a small Bible and sighed to herself. *Lord, are my eyes deceiving me, or have I awoken from my long quiet sleep into a nightmare of devils and clowns? Give me the strength to understand your ways. Lord, give me the strength!*

Next to Ruth, the survivalists' jaws dropped, unsure if they had heard correctly. *Sixteen trillion dollars?* Stirred by Judge Bacchus's mention of suffering, the bald-headed Buddhists began to meditate silently while the twins jibber jabbered gruntingly into each other's ear. Judge Bacchus continued. "First we'll hear from the Plaintiffs. I invite their lawyer, Attorney Otto Griebel to take the floor. Mr. Griebel, your opening remarks please."

Otto Griebel stood up from his table. He patted his navy suit jacket and swiped a hand through his fabulous hair. His baby blue handkerchief sparkled in unison with his tie. Arthur and the gang watched him take the center of the room from their seats in the front row. Across the aisle behind the Public Defender, the blonde Bombshells squirmed and whispered to the man with the parrot, *handsome, isn't he?*

Otto stood confidently in the center of the courtroom. He smiled at the cameras. He winked at the stenographer. He spun around on his heels and shot people with his hands; Miss Telemundo, Fox News, CBS, Anton Brown, the twins, and lastly, dear old Ruth. Ruth looked Otto up and down. *Smarmy,* she thought. She shook her head and prayed, *Lord, when I was in my coma, I thought, 'this is your test', but I see now that it was only the beginning. Like the righteous Lot, Lord, give me the strength to persevere.*

Otto addressed the jury "Ladies and gentlemen of the jury, how are you doing today?" He paused to smile and then continued. "Fine, I hope. Over the course of these proceedings, I intend to show you how everyone is responsible for the dismal conditions under which we live today and how because of everyone, society isn't what it used to be. In order to right everyone's wrongs, it's true, we're asking for a substantial amount of money. But this lawsuit isn't about the money. It's about man's dignity. It's about how everyone keeps holding everyone back. It's about how everyone has ignored the rights of our least advantaged and about the bleak future everyone is building for our children. This trial is about our politics, which are meant to heal us, but are only making us sicker, and the destruction that we're doing to the Earth and the grave that we're digging for our children. As a result of everyone's gross negligence, our politicians, corporations, spiritual leaders, and even our neighbors have been allowed to cause us irreparable harm. All we're asking for is the return of our dignity, financially speaking."

"Before this trial is over, you will hear from Arthur Jay, a corporate man who just can't get ahead, Tyrone Jenkins, who can't even get started, Greta Gernhart, who got to the end only to have it all taken away. Then aspiring artist Jackie Lim will take the stand, followed by Doctor of Ecology, Gustavo Jeremiah, and none other than former Congresswoman May Farleigh. By the end of their combined testimony it should be evident that as a result of everyone's gross negligence, we are all suffering in one way or another and restitution is due. Thank you."

Otto sat down. The Public Defender, dressed in loose beige pants and an oversized coat, stood up. His hair was thin, black and combed over, held in place with a thick sticky smear of glistening pomade across his shiny forehead. The Public Defender shuffled to the center of the courtroom and addressed the jury. "People of the jury. As I will show you over the course of these proceedings, everyone is not guilty. While the Plaintiff would like you to believe that our corporations, politicians, doctors and media have all hung us out to dry, and everyone has somehow allowed them to do so through complete lack of interest or personal responsibility, I will show you that everyone is not guilty." The Public Defender paused for dramatic effect. " How can everyone be guilty when everyone else is? And who can blame them?" The Public Defender smiled to himself. *Enough said,* he thought. *The state pays me either way, anyway, win or lose.* He raised his eyebrows and glanced around the room. Then he shuffled back to his seat and returned to his newspaper.

Judge Bacchus addressed the court. "Attorney Griebel, Public Defender, thank you. Now that we have heard the opening remarks, Mr. Gricbel, please call your first witness." Otto Griebel stood up again and walked to the center of the room. He looked like a million bucks in his brown leather loafers and slim suit. His toothy smile reflected in the stenographer's twinkling eyes. "I call Arthur Jay to the stand."

V

Arthur Jay Testifies

Arthur Jay stood up from the bench. Blood rushed to his head. He felt a swoon. All eyes were on him in the courtroom and over the airwaves. Butterflies fluttered in his stomach. Tyrone glared at him skeptically. *Don't screw this up*, Arthur told himself. The flashbulbs flashed hot on his face as he walked the line to the witness stand. Beads of sweat formed on his forehead. He hadn't felt nerves like this since he asked foxy Roxy Mendez to the junior prom. What was he afraid of? The cameras? The questions? He had practiced enough with Otto. *Nothing to it but to do it,* he told himself. Ten long steps and Arthur Jay was standing in the witness stand swearing an oath to tell the truth, the whole truth and nothing but the truth. Then he sat down, adjusted his jacket and took a deep breath.

Otto smiled confidently at Arthur, and started the questioning. "Welcome, Mr. Jay. Please, if you wouldn't mind, would you please tell the court a little bit about yourself."

"Well," said Arthur, "my name is Arthur Jay. I'm thirty-four years old. I work as an engineer and I feel like I can't get ahead. I graduated from college twelve years ago and I've been working ever since. I get two weeks of vacation each year, and when I look into the future, all I see is more work. I have credit card debt, a car loan and a mortgage. I only just paid off my student loans, and after I pay my bills every month, I barely manage to save a dime. Every time I do, a pipe bursts at my house or my car breaks down. I feel like a slave to this lifestyle. All this driving is making me fat, and it feels like I'm always mowing my lawn."

"Mr. Jay," Otto interrupted. "Thank you. You've told me several times that you feel trapped by your lifestyle. If that's the case, why not change?"

"Well, I suppose I'm just trying to meet expectations. I grew up middle class, and have an obligation to remain middle class, and a middle class man ought to have a house and a car. People would judge me if I didn't. Plus dating is hard when you ride the bus."

The court chuckled at Arthur's comment, except for Tyrone who starred at him coldly. Otto asked again, "But Mr. Jay, why not an apartment then?"

Arthur replied, "That's a good question, but it's not that simple. You know, I bought my house six years ago. Every year it's something. The minute I moved in, the boiler failed, the driveway buckled and my shower leaked. I found rotten siding and I had a fly infestation. I don't know if I've spent more time doing my own amateur repairs or waiting for contractors who never show up. You ought to sec the bathroom sink I hung last year. It's so crooked; the soap keeps sliding off. But I don't have time to redo it, and I don't have the money or patience to hire a plumber. I'd love to move into an apartment, and let someone else do the landscaping, but I've poured so much money and emotion into my house, the thought of moving is overwhelming."

"Mr. Jay," Otto asked. "From what I hear, it sounds as if you find the middle class lifestyle stressful."

"Being middle-class *is* stressful! It's not easy living up to everyone's expectations. Some days, I'd rather be bohemian, but I need the health insurance."

"Mr. Jay," Otto asked, "do you think it's fair to say that your suffering is a result of expectations? Is it possible that you're trying too hard to live up to society's expectations, and therefore, everyone's expectations are at the root of your suffering?" At the second mention of suffering, the Buddhists, with their eyes closed, deep in thought, perked up their ears.

"Absolutely. My suffering is absolutely a result of everyone's expectations. A middle class man is expected to have a house and a car, and live on a quiet cul-de-sac. My mother was a middle class lady, and she expects me to be a proper middle-class man, but I just want to grow my beard and write poetry. I'd rather have time and no money than neither time nor money. Yet some days it feels like the latter, and the harder I work, the less of both I seem to have."

"Thank you Mr. Jay. It's clear to me that everyone's expectations have caused you some amount of hardship, but what about your own expectations? Are they not also causing you hardship?"

"Well yes," Arthur replied. "My expectations are absolutely causing me hardship. I expected a lot more from this life. For that I blame my mother. She never beat me. Like Siddhartha, I thought life would be easy street and chocolate cake, until I stepped out of the comfort of my parents' nest and into the real world.

Until I got a job, I had no idea how awful adulthood was. I wish someone would have told me sooner."

"Mr. Jay. Can you tell me a little bit more about your job?"

"Yes I can. I work a nine to five, although I'm usually there past seven. I get up every morning at six AM. I shower, shave, eat a bowl of cereal and head off into traffic. As soon as I get into my car, everyone and their mother is in my way. People cut me off. Some knowingly. Some while talking on their phones. Every day I'm more and more convinced that I'll die in a fiery car crash on my way to work. The last thing I'll hear is a loud crunch and some imbecile on talk radio talking about traffic or celebrity gossip, as I bleed out on the freeway.

"After risking life and limb on the interstate, Mondays thru Fridays, I get the pleasure of spending a minimum of eight hours in a windowless cubicle, breathing recycled office air, while I fritter and waste the hours, responding to emails and writing technical reports."

Arthur was on a roll now. Oblivious to the cameras, the jurors or Tyrone's intense stare, he carried on. "Last year, I did a great job saving the company money in our cost reduction initiatives. My ideas will save the company one million dollars each year. As recognition for my hard work, I was promoted. My boss said to me, 'Arthur, you did a great job. I'm giving you a promotion in advance. You should see something nice in your raise at the end of the year'. But come time for our annual cost of living adjustments, the CEO declared a cost cutting initiative of his own. That's right, layoffs and a wage freeze. While I got nothing for my hard work but another year in the salt mine, his bonus doubled to twenty five million dollars. It's ridiculous. People are getting laid off, wages are frozen and the CEO gets stock options? Another million for a multi-millionaire isn't nearly as useful as another grand for a man like me. But while my CEO is swimming in wealth, all my hard work gets me is more hard work, and a *better luck next year*." Arthur looked annoyed.

Otto interjected. "Mr. Jay, I get the sense that this arrangement offends you." This was it. This was the queue that Arthur was waiting for. He and Otto had practiced this part for weeks. Arthur Jay stood up and pounded his palms on the witness box.

"You're darn right this arrangement offends me. I work day after day trying to sustain the middle class dream, trying to live up to everyone's expectations, but fighting against everyone at the same time, trying to get to work faster, so I can work faster, and make money faster. But for what? A bigger house, and a bigger car? I can't keep up with the ones I have now. And despite knowing how ridiculous it all is, I still stubbornly tread water, while people like my CEO are racing around me in speedboats.

"In the thousand years since the dark ages, nothing has changed. The common man toils while the lords live in luxury. We've replaced kings with politicians and nobility with CEO's but the power system is no different. We've all just been hoodwinked into thinking that we're free by big screen TVs and fast cars. I don't know if it's serfdom or slavery, but either way, everyone's guilty for taking it without even realizing it. Where are the politicians in all of this? Where are the voters? Where are the unions?" Then Arthur Jay slammed his fist on the railing of the witness stand. "Where is the justice?"

The frantic clickety-clack of stenographer Mary Jane Reefer's typing came to a stop. The courtroom was silent except for the sound of Mary Jane cracking her knuckles, just warming up. The red lights of the cameras were all focused on Arthur. He realized now that he was sweating profusely. He wiped his brow with the back of his palm. He could see that sweat stains were creeping through his yellow shirt where his stomach pushed against the buttons.

Otto turned to Judge Bacchus. "No further questions, Your Honor." Judge Bacchus addressed the Public Defender. "Your witness." The Public

Defender dropped his pen and stood up. "No further questions, Your Honor." He sat back down and returned to his newspaper. Arthur couldn't tell, but it looked like he was working on the crossword puzzle.

Without much pause, Otto Griebel addressed the court. "I'd like to call my next witness, Tyrone Jenkins." Arthur stepped out of the witness stand. He felt elation. He was done. A feeling of incredible relief swept over him from his head to his toes. His part was over. He said what he had to say. Now he could sit back and watch the rest of the show. He walked back to the bench.

Tyrone Jenkins, born of the ghetto and to die of the ghetto, gave Arthur the stink eye. They bumped shoulders as they traded places. Tyrone, all in black in baggy pants with a blousy button down shirt and a black tie, his hair braided in tight cornrows, swaggered cool as a cucumber to the witness stand. On his way he nodded to the stenographer, made a peace sign to the cameras and addressed Bailiff Anton Brown. "Sup brother?" Anton turned his head and adjusted his belt, unimpressed. As Tyrone settled into the witness stand, Otto addressed him. "Good afternoon, Mr. Jenkins. Thank you for joining us this morning. "

"My pleasure Mr. Griebel. But before we start the questioning, I have something I need to say."

"What is that Mr. Jenkins?"

Inspired by Arthur's daring testimony, Tyrone veered for a moment from the script to speak straight from the heart. "Fuck Arthur Jay."

VI

Tyrone Jenkins

"Objection!" yelled Arthur. Judge Bacchus swung his gavel. "Sustained! Mr. Jenkins, this is not a kangaroo court. I'll kindly ask you to keep your language professional."

"Sorry, Your Honor." Tyrone replied. "What I meant to say was, forget Mr. Jay. Seriously. He's got a lot of nerve, comin in here and blabbin his mouth about some kind of slavery."

Otto smiled and laughed coolly. "Mr. Jenkins, you don't mean that do you?"

"Yea. I do. He's got a lot of nerve comin down from the suburbs, livin in his nice house, drivin a car, wearin fancy clothes, and talkin about sufferin or some stupid somethin. If you want to know about sufferin, all you need to do is ask." Otto, now looking serious, addressed Tyrone, "Mr. Jenkins, would you please tell the court a little bit about yourself."

Tyrone started. "Well, to be truthful it's a long story. You see, I was born forty-three years ago to a wonderful woman with some real problems. My mother was a single mother and I was her only child. I never met my father. He was in jail in some other city somewhere.

"As a single mom, my mom had a hard time bringin me up. She was young and broke and on her own. She used drugs, you know, to cope. Her habit was so bad, the first words out of my mouth were 'pass the pipe'. Needless to say, my environment wasn't, *enriching*. I didn't eat regular meals. I didn't have no role models. One year I ain't even had no winter coat. I mean, the way I was raised, I was more like a wild animal than anything else. Ain't nobody could tell me what to do. By the time I got to school I was nothin but trouble. Teachers couldn't teach me a lick. I acted out in class. I fought in the schoolyard. I stole candy from the drug store. I even sold that candy. I made a pretty penny sellin stolen lollipops for a quarter. That's a hundred percent profit, Baby!"

Tyrone smiled at his early memory. But then his face soured. "Things got worse for me as I got older. By the time I was sixteen I was still in the sixth grade. I only made it that far because the teachers were embarrassed for me and didn't want to hold me back no more. At that point, I stopped goin to school and spent my days just hangin out and hustlin on the street, and to be honest, it was a lot better than bein in school. I woke up when I wanted. I hung out at the park. I got fresh air. I had friends and acquaintances. But the good times weren't to last. We were too stupid, always schemin some new way to make money. We sold a little weed. We stole rims. Once we jumped this dude in the park, but it ended up a fight and there wasn't that much in his wallet, so we didn't do that again. We would have sold more drugs, but we just didn't have the capital to get into the game. Any profits we might have made, we smoked. So finally, we got the idea to rob a jewelry store, to make some real money.

"My boy Slim explained it perfect. He had it all figured out. He had this jewelry store cased solid. Every day, the owner left the store last and he always left by the back door. All we had to do was strong-arm him before he could lock the door. Then we would tie him up, and take all the jewelry. I mean, damn. Slim was talkin about a million dollars in jewels. A million dollars!"

Tyrone grinned widely and shook his head. His eyes were bright with dollar signs. "We were amped up. Now, no one was supposed to get hurt. Sure the owner might be scared if we tied him up and all, but we weren't plannin to do him bad. It was meant to be a victimless crime. The insurance would have made him even anyhow, financially speaking. But you see, what happened is, things didn't turn out so well.

"It was about six o'clock on a winter's day. It was dark already and the parkin lot was dark. Me, Slim and our boy Jimmy were waitin in the bushes with ski masks on when the owner came out. He was dressed like an old fashioned private eye in a beige overcoat, and he had a brief case. There was a security light shinin on him over the door. We had to be quick to muscle him and get inside without too much noise. Now, we didn't mean no harm, honest. It was meant to be a victimless crime. So when we jumped this dude, we were surprised to see that he could fight. I mean he was like a ninja or somethin. Slim came up first, but this dude just smacked Slim with his brief case, and tripped him with his leg. Slim flipped up in the air and landed flat on his back. Then the man kicked him in the ribs. Jimmy tried to swing a punch, but the man blocked it with his forearm. Then he grabbed Jimmy by the head and spun him into the brick wall. I lunged at the dude. He pulled off my mask and punched me in the nose. I couldn't believe it! He was like Segal, Van Damme and Chuck Norris all in one. Me, Jimmy and Slim split fast in three ways.

"Two days later, I'm in the park over by the elementary school, doin my thing. There's one other guy in the park who keeps starin at me like he knew me, but I didn't know him so I paid him no mind. Now I had some weed on me, and I was waitin to meet up with Slim. Finally, Slim shows up, limpin like a sucker from that fight at the jewelry store, and he's chucklin all about it, and laughin at my black eye and Slim says, 'I ain't doin no more jewelry stores no time soon'. And that's when we got handcuffed. Turns out the dude in the park was undercover, and he did recognize me! A camera outside the jewelry store had video from when that dude ripped off my mask." Tyrone looked dumbfounded. "I mean, what are the odds?"

Otto shook his head. "Mr. Jenkins. That's unbelievable. Please tell the court what happened next."

"Well, they threw the book at me. Attempted robbery. Aggravated assault. Trespassin. Plus the weed I had on me that day in the park, which was even worse because I was next to a school. Drug free zone or somethin. Oh, and I cursed that officer good. They threatened assault of an officer for one curse too many. Long story short, I was given fifteen years with a chance of parole after six. But I spent eight in the joint. Now that I'm a felon, I can't get no job, I can't vote and my prospects are bleak. What I want to know is, where's my second chance?"

Otto shook his head sympathetically and then asked, "Mr. Jenkins, while you were in prison, did you have time to think?"

"Yes sir, I did."

"What did you think about Mr. Jenkins, while you were in prison?"

"Well, after the sadness and the anger passed, I stopped blamin myself, and started to look deeper into the cause of my decisions. That's when I realized; it wasn't my fault that I was in prison. It was everyone's fault."

"Mr. Jenkins," Otto asked, "please explain to the court how everyone was responsible for your incarceration."

"It's simple. Whether people are discriminatin, or just shruggin they shoulders at the system, lives like mine inevitable."

"How so Mr. Jenkins?" Otto asked.

Tyrone answered, "Well, you can blame slavery. You can blame Jim Crow. They got this whole ghetto machinery spinnin in the first place. But what I finally realized after all my thinkin, is that that ain't relevant. What started this whole thing spinnin don't matter no more. The point isn't how we got here, but that we got here. And this is where we are…we're livin in a world in which too many children grow up in broken homes, with broken dreams. When a child's first broken words are *shut up,* and he's lucky to eat breakfast twice a week, he's startin this race from a mile back.

"Even worse, without role models, not only are these children startin the race a mile back, but there ain't even no one to tell them that they in a race in the first place. By the time these children realize they in a race, they realize there ain't no way they ever gonna win. So some of them cheat. Some of them quit. Some of them get angry. And this anger? It leads to violence, and the violence leads to more anger. And the ghetto machinery just keeps spinnin around, spittin out one disadvantaged child after another. Police brutality, incarceration rates, drug abuse. All of these are symptoms of the ghetto disease, except these symptoms just make the anger worse, and the disease stronger. And the machinery feeds off that disease, like a cancer."

Otto interrupted Tyrone. "Mr. Jenkins. If the ghetto is a disease, what is the cure?"

"Attorney Griebel, the cure is obvious. The cure is education. If all children learned to read and write, and found ways to solve problems without anger; if all children had healthy meals at school, good teachers, and the right role models; then they would get good jobs, and live good lives, and raise good children. But this country would rather spend trillions on bombs, than billions on schools. And whether it's people like Arthur Jay, obsessed about they own bizness, talkin about how they can't get ahead when they already ahead, or it's backwarded politicians fightin for the rich instead of the poor, investors that profit from prisons, or all the people who would rather pretend that racism is dead now that a black man's been president, everyone's guilty."

Tyrone crossed his arms, and shook his head disgustedly. Otto addressed Judge Bacchus. "No further questions, Your Honor."

Judge Bacchus looked at the Public Defender who looked up from his crossword. He was making progress, but was presently stuck on 19-across. Five letters, ends in "n". *Never the _____shall meet.* "No further questions, Your Honor."

Tyrone Jenkins stepped out of the witness box and sauntered back to the Plaintiff's row. Arthur Jay squeezed himself in, to let Tyrone pass unhindered. "Sorry," Tyrone said. "It's nothin personal. I'm sure you a straight dude. But seriously though. You got some nerve talkin about slavery and shit."

VII

First Recess

After Tyrone's testimony, Judge Bacchus swung his gavel and called for recess. He hopped off the bench and walked to his chambers where a bottle of warm merlot waited for him. *Just one glass*, he told himself. *Just one.* Anton Brown held the door for him, as Judge Bacchus left the courtroom.

Over in the media booth, all of the cameras' lights were dark. The stations paused for commercial. Their talking heads, and ticker tapes went still for a moment so that Viagra and Cialis could compete for market share. Chevy aired a touching commercial about freedom and cars. A rock music photomontage of everyone drinking Coca-Cola warmed everyone's hearts. Apple, McDonalds, GE, Amazon; even the Koch brothers chimed in to hawk their brand in exchange for premiums higher than the Super Bowl. When the advertisements stopped, the ticker tapes started up again. *Outburst in the Courtroom. Arthur Jay insulted.* The talking heads queued up Tyrone's cursing, to a slow motion of Arthur's reaction and fist banging objection. Little pieces of white spittle could be seen shooting from his lips.

Across the room in the jury box, the twins played rock-paper-scissors, while the Buddhists meditated deeply on the idea of suffering and its cause, which so far seemed to be the theme of the trial. The survivalists reclined with their feet up on the rail of the jury box. The big one scratched his scraggly beard. He caught his finger in a knot, tugged something loose and flicked it at his friend. Survivalist number two was asleep, as he had been for the last hour, reclining lazily in his seat, snoring quietly like a dog with his eyes open. Number three spoke to Ruth.

"How'd they find you?" he asked. In her sweet island accent, Ruth answered. "Find me? Young man, they done took me from the arms of the Lord into this devil's playground. I was in a coma until just this morning. Defeated by a wily spider they told me, and laid up in a hospital bed for eight months I was. Then I woke up, and won't you know it, before I could remember my own name, I was eating a banana in the lobby of this here courthouse and made a witness of this tomfoolery. Everyone versus Everyone? This must be some sort of a joke. I haven't even had a chance to call my sons and tell them that I'm ok." Ruth crossed her arms and *harrumphed*. The survivalist shook his head. "I thought I had it bad. But ma'am, that's something awful."

"Well, don't you know, the Lord works in mysterious ways. Now tell me son, how did you and your friends get mixed up in this here business?"

"Actually, sort of the same story, in that we were taken here against our will and told that it was our civic duty to sit on this jury, or else. But it all started much further back. Many years ago, almost two decades in fact, my two friends and I realized that the modern world was no longer for us. Yes, it was comfortable. Yes, we had our jobs. We had food and roofs over our heads. Life was simple and there was plenty. But living every day waiting for time to pass at work, wishing the clock would tick faster, just to race back home and wait for the weekend to begin, began to feel meaningless. The only thing we can never get back is time. To waste so much time waiting, began to weigh on us. We craved lives of simplicity. It's not that we shunned work. We wanted to be busy. We just didn't want to be busy the way we were, so we decided to live life by our own rules. We purchased supplies and moved off the grid.

"It was springtime almost eighteen years ago when we hitched our way to Yellowstone National Park. We arrived with clothes, tools, and a small supply of seeds and provisions. Immediately we set off toward the hills to establish a camp. We settled by a lake. We built a hut with a stone chimney. We fished and caught small game with nets when we could. We planted carrots and radish. We collected berries and edible greens. It wasn't easy. In fact sometimes it was tough, but we were living on the edge, making decisions that mattered. We were cold, wet and hungry, but we were alive. By the time winter came, we had discovered good fishing grounds and established a means to preserve our catch by smoking and drying. And though it was a long, hard winter, and many times we questioned our motives, spring eventually came and life was good again. We learned from the last year's mistakes and the next winter went smoother, and the next one even more so. Eighteen years passed in the blink of an eye.

"Then, just a few days ago, the three of us were discovered close to a logging camp and arrested for trespassing. The army came in and quarantined us. They told us to do as they said and sit on this jury or they'd make us disappear forever. So frankly, I don't care what happens with this trial. As soon as we can, we're getting out of here. Quickly and quietly, if you know what I mean."

"Amen to that," Ruth said. At the front of the courtroom, there was a knock. Anton Brown spoke, "All rise, the Honorable Judge Bacchus." Mary-Jane Reefer checked her wristwatch and began to type. Anton opened a door and Judge Bacchus entered the courtroom. He wiped his lips with his bare hand and stepped up to the bench. His black robes fluttered. He swung his gavel and declared with a slight slur, "Court is in session." Then he smiled. His teeth were red.

VIII

Greta Gernhart

The next contestant to testify was great Greta Gernhart, age 61, widowed. Greta lived across town from Arthur, on the second floor of a three family house. She was forced to move there three years earlier after her husband's medical bills forced them into bankruptcy. By the time the funeral was over, all she had left to her name was a futon, a backpack, a color television and a Chihuahua named Charlie. Her daughter Karleen, her only child, lived far away in Seattle, a whole day's travel by air.

After Judge Bacchus swung his gavel, Otto called Greta to the witness stand. The cameras turned and zoomed in on Greta. She had been calm all morning, but all of a sudden, she felt a sharp pain in her chest. *Not again*, she thought fearfully. Greta shifted her weight and the pain moved. It moved into her throat where it grew hot. *Brrrrrpp.* Greta exhaled. The smell of sour cream and onions floated past Tyrone and Arthur. It floated across the aisle and settled like smog upon the Bombshells and the one-eyed man. The parrot on the one-eyed man's shoulder squawked.

Exhaling with relief, Greta shook her wide hips and wiggled her rear end into position. With her hands on her knees she pressed forcefully and stood up. With a huff, she grabbed her cane and her back and lumbered forward to the witness stand. In a light colored muumuu with purple and gold flowers, great Greta Gernhart placed one swollen palm on the Bible, another on her heart, and swore the oath in a sweet and lovely mid-western brogue.

"I swear to tell the truth, the whole truth and nothing but the truth," she declared. Judge Bacchus addressed her. "Thank you. Mrs. Gernhart, please be seated." Otto positioned himself in the center of the courtroom. "Mrs. Gernhart, thank you for joining us today. How are you feeling?"

"I'm well, thank you," Greta said matter-of-factly. Otto replied, "Mrs. Gernhart, that's good to hear, because I understand that you've had some medical trouble as of late."

"Yes sir, that's correct."

"For the court's record, please tell us about your recent difficulty."

"Mr. Griebel, with pleasure. You see, it all started about seven months ago around Christmas. My daughter Karleen was visiting with my grandson Geoffrey. We were having a delightful time, playing games and watching movies, and eating turkey and ham, and stuffing, and gravy. And there was pie, with whipped cream of course. For almost a week we just hung around the living room, relaxing and eating leftovers. You know how the holidays go."

"I certainly do," Otto replied, but Greta just blustered on. "Now, because I had been eating so much, I wasn't paying much attention to this pain in my chest. *A little indigestion,* I told myself. Plus Karleen and Geoffrey were in town and I didn't want to interrupt the fun. But, eventually all good things come to an end, and my babies had to go home. Karleen's a paralegal, you see, in Seattle. She lives there with her husband Bill, who I don't much care for. But at least he's got a job, and they give him good insurance. Anyhow, Karleen was leaving. She doesn't get much time off from her work, and she didn't want to leave Bill alone on New Years. Plus, her ticket was already booked.

"It was a long drive to the airport and Karleen insisted on paying for a cab, but I wouldn't let her waste the money. Besides, driving meant another hour with her and Geoffrey. So we got into my wagon, and took off into the night. It was a long ride but we made it without any trouble. I kissed my babies good-bye in the airport terminal and hugged them hard. Then I was alone again.

"I drove home, listening to Christmas carols on repeat. As soon as I got in, I gave my dog Charlie a big old hug. He licked the tears from my face. I rubbed his belly, and you know, I forgot about Karleen, and I forgot about the pain in my chest for a little while. But as the night went on, the pain grew worse. I was hoping it was just gas, but every time I thought it couldn't get worse, it did. So around midnight, after it got so bad I could hardly breathe, I decided to drive to the walk-in clinic. I probably should have called an ambulance, but who knows what that would have cost.

"By the time I got to the doctor's office, the pain was overwhelming, but at the reception desk, a young woman stopped me in my tracks. Without even looking at me, she just said, 'insurance card'. And wouldn't you know it, in my haste I realized I left it at home.

"I said, 'ma'am, I don't have it on me, and I think I'm going to faint.' Then she handed me a clipboard and a pen. At that point, she still hadn't looked me in the face, and she said, "Fill this out." After filling out my name, medical history, family medical history, known allergies, and credit score in block letters, she told me to take a seat. 'The doctor will be with you she said.' She never even looked at me!

"I was sitting in that waiting room for what seemed like an eternity, and the pain just kept getting worse. There was a fish tank bubbling in the corner, but I didn't see any fish, just a lot of algae, and there was a young man sitting next to it. He appeared to be asleep. I flipped through the periodicals to try and distract myself, but neither medical journals nor celebrity gossip could quell my discomfort. I looked at my watch. It was already two in the morning. I thought I was going to die when a nurse finally called me to the consultation room where she took my vitals and asked me to get changed. Then finally, I was sitting on the doctor's table on that slippery wax paper, in that foolish robe, when the pain got so bad that I blacked out and fell off the table. The doctor found me face down on the linoleum, with my full moon shining."

Greta looked sad. She shook her head, "How embarrassing." Otto interrupted her for a moment. "Mrs. Gernhart, that's not the end of your story is it?"

"No, Mr. Griebel, it isn't. As it turns out, I was having a heart attack and I needed emergency surgery. I woke up the next day after the operation, but I was in such a pain, and the narcotics were so strong, that I slept for another day and then some. By the time I came to my senses, it was almost two full days since I left the house. I panicked. *Charlie,* I thought, *he's all alone!* There weren't any nurses around or anyone else in my room. It took me two hours to get someone on the phone. I didn't have my neighbors' cell phone numbers. My deadbeat landlord wasn't answering his phone, and my only friend was away visiting her daughter for the holidays. Finally I got a hold of Karleen, god bless her. I begged her to fly back and she did. She had to call in sick and miss pay to do it, but she did it. But even still, it took her forever. My blood pressure was through the roof with worry. It took her another day and a half to get to me by train, plane and taxi, and in all that time, I couldn't get anyone else on the phone. Even the police told me it wasn't an emergency. Not an emergency?!" Greta looked infuriated.

"I've never felt more alone or helpless. Finally, Karleen ran into the room with all her luggage. I kissed her and gave her my house keys and told her to hurry. Charlie was depending on it!" At this point, Greta became upset. The memory of it all was too much. She began to sob. Otto spoke softly to her. "Mrs. Gernhart, please tell the court what happened next." Greta snorted hard. "Well, you know, Charlie is really my only companion. He was alone at that point for four days. My weakened heart was already bursting from the thought of life without Charlie. He's all I have. Then finally, the phone rang. I was afraid to answer it, but I did. I couldn't hear what Karleen was saying, but in the background, I heard barking. Charlie was alive! He was ok, that little devil. He survived on toilet water and trash, God bless him."

The court heaved a sigh of relief. Everyone exhaled in unison. Stenographer Mary-Jane Reefer paused from typing and wiped away a tear. The one-eyed man and the Bombshells clasped hands and smiled at each other. Ruth shook her head in confusion. Then Otto resumed his questioning. "Mrs. Gernhart, that isn't the end of your story, now is it?"

"No, Mr. Griebel, it isn't. I spent three more days in the hospital with Karleen by my side. And thank goodness she was there or I would have died from bad food or out of sheer neglect. As it was, I almost died anyhow. For three days, I didn't improve. I actually got worse. By January first, they had to put me under for a second surgery to *improve* the results of the first surgery and treat a bacterial growth. Super bacteria or something. After the follow-on surgery, I started to get better. After another three days, I went home to Charlie, and Karleen went back to work.

"Four weeks later I got two bills in the mail for fifteen grand a piece. I called my insurance company, and insisted that there was a mistake. They assured me that in fact there was no mistake. The first fifteen was for the first surgery before the last of December, and the second fifteen was for the second surgery after the first of January, including room and board of course. Those dirty rats got me for the full deductible in both years."

Greta looked confused and briefly overwhelmed. Otto inquired further. "Mrs. Gernhart, what happened next?"

"Well, and I'm not making this up, because I'm under oath, but I had a second heart attack. The hospital bills nearly killed me. I went right back to the hospital!" Then Greta smiled. "But the joke's on them. I already reached the annual deductible, so I won't pay those crooks a dime for my second heart attack. Ha ha!" Greta chuckled and then looked serious again. "But seriously, I worked too long and hard to be put in this situation. If you ask me, everyone's guilty for letting these doctors and insurers get away with murder. I owe thirty thousand dollars for my misfortune. If this trial doesn't pan out, I'll have to move in with Karleen. I'm not sure who's more upset about it, me or my son-in-law, Bill."

Otto looked at Judge Bacchus. "No further questions, Your Honor."

IX

Aspiring Artist Jackie Lim

The Public Defender had no questions for Greta. He was stuck on the top corner of his crossword puzzle. He wasn't sure if 16-DOWN, "*Pun's accomplice*" was 'IRONY' or 'CRONY', and 14-ACROSS, three letters, "*F in Athens*", wasn't ringing a bell.

Across the room, Jackie Lim rocked nervously on the bench. She was next. Her gaze was fixed on her black boots when Otto called her to the stand. In the media box, the cameras zoomed in on Jackie. Her bright red lips matched the streak of red in her jet-black hair. Around the world, television viewers fell in love with her pouty face.

Jackie stood up and looked at Greta with big eyes. "You can do it," Greta whispered. Jackie squeezed past Greta, and down the row toward the aisle. Tyrone winked and made a kissy face as Jackie passed. Arthur tried not to stare.

On television sets around the world, in living rooms, bars and sidewalks, the twenty-four hour news channels broadcast a split screen. To the right of Jackie's face, screens across the globe displayed a short biography in five bullets.

Aspiring Artist Jackie Lim.
Age 24.
Musician.
Plays Piano, Guitar and Sings.
Alleged nymphomaniac.

On the airwaves, the talking heads chattered about Jackie's character, her background and her sex life. Three hacked images of topless Jackie in a hot tub, stolen from her cell phone, were broadcast with censored black bars to crowds of applauding viewers.

The courtroom was oblivious to all of this. Otto began his questioning. "Miss Lim, thank you for testifying today. As we've heard from Arthur, Tyrone and Greta, getting ahead isn't easy. But as you and I have discussed, you're not trying to get ahead are you?"

"No, Mr. Griebel, I'm not trying to get ahead. I'm trying to get to the top. Go big or go home, if you know what I mean." Otto smiled. "I know exactly what you mean, Miss Lim. But to the top of what?"

"To the top of the pops, of course." Jackie replied. Otto laughed facetiously. "And how do you intend to get to the top of the pops?"

"Through music, of course. My band's name is *Ras Beats.* We play a mix of reggae, hardcore and hip-hop. I play guitar, piano and work the mike, depending on the composition. My band mates, and best friends, Tom and Bill play rhythm on bass and drums."

Otto asked, "Miss Lim, I know you've been involved in music your whole life. Can you tell the court about that?"

"That's correct. I started playing piano at the age of four, and was singing by six. I was born with the gift of rhythm and tone. As a child, I attended a music school full time. Music has always been my passion. Now I'm trying to live my dream."

"And how is that dream coming along?"

"It's coming. Slowly I think. We're not where I thought we'd be after nine years together. But we're booked most weekends. And we have a demo tape that's been circling for about a year now."

"Jackie Lim, isn't that just fantastic!" Otto exclaimed.

"It's good, but it's not enough. I'm still living in my parents' basement. If I don't get a deal soon, I'll have to get a real job. Can you imagine?"

Otto smiled. Jackie was sitting up confidently in the witness stand, full of sass and pride. Otto asked, "I imagine that you've sent your demo tape to various record labels and music agents. Can you tell me how that has gone?"

Jackie frowned a little. "About a year ago, we finished the tape, and started shopping it to producers and agents. The band and I spent days, and weeks, and then months, waiting for feedback. We must have sent a hundred copies of our demo tape without a single letter back in the mail."

Jackie shook her head. Then she picked it up and smiled. "But then just a month ago, I heard back from Pirate Booty records. I was actually brought in for an interview."

"Jackie," Otto exclaimed. "That's really fantastic!"

"Sort of, Mr. Griebel. Although if I wasn't under oath, you might not believe what the agent had to say to me."

"You are under oath. Please tell the court what the agent said to you."

"He told me my music was fine, but my body wasn't ready. He said, 'Call me when you put three more inches on your hips. A flat ass ain't marketable.' He told me to do some squats or get on the stair machine. Then he escorted me out of his office."

The court was outraged. The Bombshells in the front row shook their heads in disgust. Their bleached blonde hair tossed about as they stomped their feet with repulsion. *Uggh,* they shouted. In the back rows, the public cried with outrage. *Pig! Men! Sexist jerk. What an outrage!*

Judge Bacchus swung his gavel, and knocked it loudly. "Order in the court!" He yelled. "Order in the court!"

Otto looked Jackie in the eyes and solemnly asked, "Miss Lim, how did that make you feel?" Jackie's face lit up. "It made me feel great Mr. Griebel. Finally, a glimmer of hope! I've been working out six days a week since. I have a follow up interview this Friday."

In the jury box, Ruth crossed her heart. *Poor lost child*, she thought to herself. *Lord, give this girl the strength to do right!*

Despite the thrill of hope, Jackie sighed. "C'est la vie, though. Right now a door is open, but in reality, I'm still living in my parent's basement. Gigs don't pay enough, and gas is expensive." Jackie stuck out her lower lip and pouted.

Otto sympathized, "It's not easy, is it Jackie?"

"No, Mr. Griebel it's not. Breaking into music is a catch twenty-two. You have to be popular to get on the radio, but you have to be on the radio to get popular. Without a golden ticket, chances are slim."

Then Jackie took a deep breath and hit the high note she had practiced in front of the mirror for the past eight weeks. "Music doesn't have to be good, innovative, inspirational or easy on the ears. It has to be marketable. The economics drive a two party system. Like Pepsi and Coke, the only folks left are Jay-Z and Justin Bieber. If the radio isn't playing their songs, the radio is playing their friends' songs. Consolidation and monopolization of the industry is choking the creative spirit.

"Like the corporate agro-conglomerates that conspire to overrun our fields and prairies with soybeans and GMO, corporate radio dominates the airwaves, filling it with fart jokes and the longest shelf life music that money can buy, all at the expense of the sparrows and doves and independent artists. Some day soon, the only music you'll hear will be as inspirational as corn flakes, and when that day comes, you can kiss the American spirit good bye. Whether people don't think about it, don't think it's important enough to worry about, or are content with the slop they're feeding us, everyone's guilty for the state of the radio and popular music."

Jackie nailed it. Otto cracked a smile. "Miss Lim, why do you carry on if the state of music is as bad as you say it is?" Jackie nodded coolly. "Mr. Griebel, music gives me hope for the life I want to live. I want to make a living making music, and though the odds are slim, I'd rather be in the game than on the sidelines. That's why I'll be getting up at five AM tomorrow to go to the gym."

Otto turned to Judge Bacchus. "No further questions, Your Honor." Judge Bacchus looked at the Public Defender. "Your witness," he said. The Public Defender looked up from his crossword puzzle. "No further questions, Your Honor." Then he penciled in the answer to number 82 across, six letters, third letter N, *"A bathroom fixture"*. VANITY.

X

Second Recess

After Jackie's testimony it was close to Noon. Judge Bacchus adjourned the trial for lunch and slipped away to his chamber where a half empty bottle of Merlot was waiting. Otto and the gang went to private chambers where they lunched on a platter of sandwiches and orange juice. The Bailiff led the Jury to the deliberation room where they had a similar lunch, and the audience dispersed into the courthouse to eat packed sandwiches or take something from the canteen. The Bombshells and the one-eyed man were pushing red plastic trays along the cafeteria's stainless steel counter, waiting for a helping of french-fries.

"I'm so excited," said the first Bombshell hopping up and down. She giggled and tugged on her friends arm. "Me too," said the second. "This trial is a shoe-in. The Defense isn't even trying!" She looked at the one-eyed man and smiled. "Can you believe it?"

The one-eyed man replied, "I don't see how the jury can see it any other way. It's clear. Society is bullshit. Pardon my French. Corporations, politicians, doctors and even the radio are against us. And everyone's responsible for letting things get so bad. What could be more obvious?"

The first Bombshell replied. "I Know! It's so obvious; I can't believe we didn't have this lawsuit sooner. What are you going to do with the money?"

The one-eyed man smiled. "I'll take my share and invest it in a new cage for Petey. The rest I'll set aside." He pulled a small biscuit out of his breast pocket and fed the parrot on his shoulder. "Does Petey want a cracker?" the man asked his bird in a bird voice. The parrot squawked. "Petey wants a cracker. SQUAWK. Petey wants a cracker."

The Bombshells squealed with delight. "We're going on vacation. Then we're going to buy furs! Can you believe it? We're so excited!"

XI

<u>**PhD. Gustavo Jeremiah**</u>

The public returned to their seats slowly after lunch. The one-eyed man shuffled in after the Bombshells, holding a coffee cup, yawning. Across the aisle, Arthur wrung his hands anxiously. Tyrone bopped his head to a beat that dropped silently in his head. Congresswoman Farleigh imagined herself standing at a flag draped podium declaring war against the vested interests while a mighty crowd cheered her on. Gus was stuck on a vision of himself in the African Savanna, dressed in fatigues and armed with an automatic rifle, defending a family of elephants from blank eyed poachers, when Judge Bacchus called court back into session. Gus snapped out of his daydream, at the sound of Otto's voice. Otto's confident tenor echoed in the courtroom. "I call Doctor Gustavo Jeremiah to the stand."

Immediately Gus felt his guts cave in. He hadn't felt the cameras all day, until now. Gus slid off the bench like a scared amateur into a boxing ring. He was nervous. Tyrone spoke to him like a coach in his corner. He grabbed him by the shoulders and looked him straight in the eyes. "You got this, Kid," he said. He fist-bumped Gus.

Gus took one wobbly step and grabbed onto Tyrone for balance. He pushed his glasses back up his nose. He was flushed, and his gray sweater felt warm. Gus glanced at Otto. He took a deep breath and shuffled toward center stage. A whiff of tofu and old socks followed him. Gus clenched his fists and walked determinedly to the witness stand. He scanned the room and scowled at Fox News. Then he nodded to Judge Bacchus.

Judge Bacchus spoke. "Doctor Jeremiah, do you swear to tell the truth, the whole truth and nothing but the truth?"

"I do, Your Honor," Gus replied.

"Thank you," replied Judge Bacchus. "Please be seated." Then speaking to Otto, "Mr. Griebel, please proceed." Otto looked at Gus and smiled. Gus was nervous, but he was ready. Gus would speak from the heart, and once he gained momentum, like an avalanche down a mountain, he would come roaring through.

"Doctor Jeremiah, thank you for joining us today. It's an honor to have you here. You are a professor at the local community college. Please tell the court about yourself."

"I teach ecology and other natural sciences downtown at the community college. I'm fifty-one years old. I live alone with three adopted stray cats, and a rare cactus collection. I believe humanity's first priority ought to be the care of our one and only Earth. But it seems that everyone's comfort, pleasure and ego are more important, and it drives me crazy."

Gus shook his head nervously and sucked in his lips. His pupils narrowed to pinpoints, and his nose flared as breathed in. Otto knew that look. That was Gus just warming up, so Otto egged him on. "Doctor Jeremiah, please explain to the court why you've decided to testify."

Gus's eyes grew very big behind his black glasses. "Attorney Griebel, I came here today because I can't sit idle while people commit a slow suicide through pollution and climate change. I am here today, because everyone is responsible for the grave we're digging, and the anxiety is killing me. I came to testify today on behalf of the Earth and the trees and all of the fish in the deep blue seas, and all the innocent victims of everyone's shortsighted ways."

"Doctor Jeremiah," Otto said, "we've discussed this several times in private, but maybe you can share with the court. You've often told me that you feel the weight of the world on your shoulders when it comes to the environment and man's impact on it, isn't that correct?"

"That's right. I do." Gus started to breathe slower. His face appeared calmer. "Attorney Griebel, I feel the weight of the world on my shoulders. All around me I see endless commotion, endless consumption, senseless pollution and regrettable destruction. I see too many trees cut down and too many buildings put up. I see too much sprawl and too little of God's green Earth. Though I try to hold my breath and stop time, I just see the pace of this activity picking up, speeding faster and faster every year. Every year, there are more people, more pollution and so much more momentum. I fear that we won't act until it's too late, if it's not too late already, and the thought of it is tearing me up inside.

"Maybe when the thermostat hits 145 degrees in New York City and yellow cabs are melting into the asphalt, then when it's already too late people will realize what they've done."

Gus paused to let the image sink in. The air in the court was still, and silent. Only the crinkle of a candy wrapper could be heard over the sound of Greta's heavy breathing. The audience and the jury were hypnotized by Gus's strange charisma. The wild haired survivalists and smooth-scalped Buddhists smiled inwardly, agreeing wholeheartedly with Gus's sentiment. Meanwhile, Ruth contemplated the meaning of "God's green Earth" and whether it was the same god as her God. The Siamese twins, for a change, weren't wrestling. Marla and Sharla were sitting contentedly with their hands in their lap smiling toothily. Gus, oblivious to the changed mood in the courtroom, carried on.

"When the day comes, it won't be the people that I'll feel bad for. It will be the innocent animals that I'll pity when mankind's arrogance destroys us all.

"But what makes this coming crime so heinous is that it doesn't have to be this way. Man has stood on the Moon. We have the technology to live sustainably on Earth. But the vested interests will never allow it until there's no more money to be made the old fashioned way. And the way politics works, we can't expect any help from Washington. The Democrats are too soft to tell their constituents to live within their means, and the Republicans are too hypocritical to vote for anything that might offend their donors. How can a party that loves Jesus so much, love the Earth and the poor so little? And shouldn't the church have a say in the matter? Why do the religious seem more concerned about divorce and gay marriage than the sustainability of our one and only Planet Earth? God didn't construct the Earth in six days, so that we might ruin it on the seventh."

There was no stopping Gus. Otto stood patiently at the center of the courtroom with his hands in his pockets waiting for the avalanche.

"Mr. Griebel, I try to do everything I can. All year long, I ride my bike to work. If the weather's bad, I take the bus. I always bring my lunch in reusable containers. I use both sides of every paper I print. I recycle everything. I eat only locally sourced organic produce. I don't eat meat, and I'll tell you why. I do it because I don't want the blood on my hands. All around me I see death; fallen trees, slaughtered cows, fire, smoke and fossil fuels. Around the house, if I'm not in a room, I keep the lights off. Sometimes when I am in a room, I keep the lights off. I keep the heat at fifty-five and will never own an air-conditioner. I shower rarely and use only cold water. I wear the same pair of socks and underwear for days on end, and all of my eccentricities make it hard to find a wife, but I don't know what else to do.

"I go about every day, observing the world that I live in, and I just don't understand why people seem so unconcerned. I don't understand women who drive around town all day alone in SUV's, getting their nails done and going to yoga. I don't understand hipsters who sip coffee from throw away paper cups.

I don't understand old people who know better but are too stuck in their ways. I don't understand why my co-workers throw plastic water bottles in the trash when the recycling bin is right there next to the trash. I don't understand people who aren't sad when the evening news reports that elephants are being poached to extinction and the rain forest is disappearing. I don't understand anyone that doesn't get upset when the mail is full of junk, or doesn't pity the life of a cow cut short for a schnitzel. I don't understand a Supreme Court that says corporations are people but Mother Earth is second class."

Gus was now at full speed. "I've been trying a long time to minimize my impact on the earth and live within my means, and it hurts me to see how little others are willing to sacrifice. Even though everyone has more than enough, people still refuse to get by with any less if their neighbor isn't willing to do the same, because at the end of the day, everyone's just showing off, trying to look impressive in front of their peers like peacocks in front of their hens. The thought that we live in a day and age in which we have the technological and financial means to put solar panels on every school and every public building, but choose to give oil companies tax breaks instead, makes me mourn for the decency of the human race and the dream of democracy. If this is honestly how people want to live, then I honestly wish the bird flu upon everyone. It's time to cull the human herd. There's too many awful people doing awful disgusting things and I can't take it anymore. If the government prefers war to clean water, then I say let them break out the drones. They can start with the poachers and the illegal loggers and end with everyone else. I'd rather live in the woods with the bears and the animals than spend another day with everyone here."

Gus slammed his palm on the witness stand. He made an angry frown and sat back in his chair. The courtroom was silent. Most were in shock at the drone comment. Ruth was still trying to understand what Gus meant by "God's green Earth", but the three scraggly survivalists agreed with every word he said. If Gus wanted, he could come back with them to Yellowstone. All three of them applauded softly, and gave a thumbs-up. Gus saw them nodding from the corner of his eye. He felt their support strengthening his will. He leaned forward for one last comment. His voice was loud and angry. "Whether everyone is consuming too much, conserving too little, or waiting for someone else to lead the way, everyone is guilty of spoiling this beautiful Earth for everyone else."

Gus took off his glasses and wiped his brow. He was done. Otto turned to Judge Bacchus, "No further questions, Your Honor."

Judge Bacchus looked to the Public Defender's table, but the Public Defender was gone. He had slipped away urgently during Gus's hypnotic testimony to a bathroom stall. With no one to cross-examine him, Gus stepped off the stand.

XII

Congresswoman May Farleigh

Former Congresswoman May Farleigh was the last Plaintiff that Otto would call to the stand. She looked dapper in a navy blue sports coat, with an American flag pinned to her lapel, as she sat calmly in the witness box. Her brown hair hung to her shoulders and contrasted smartly with the white of her blouse. The media's flashing cameras reflected brightly in her square glasses. Otto began his questioning.

"Mrs. Farleigh, thank you for coming here today. It's a pleasure to have you with us. As most people in the audience should know, you are a former Congresswoman, isn't that correct?"

"Mr. Griebel, first and foremost, let me say that I feel deeply humbled to be here today. It is an honor to have the opportunity to speak for everyone. I was in fact a Congresswoman from this district for twenty four years."

"Mrs. Farleigh, twenty four years is a long time to serve one's country. You must be proud of your accomplishment."

"Mr. Griebel, I am anything but proud. In fact, I am terribly ashamed. It's disgraceful how little I accomplished, how little I changed the world, and yet how profoundly politics changed me for the worse over all those years. I can tell you from first hand experience, politics is ruining everyone's life. I know because politics almost ruined mine."

Otto laughed facetiously. "Mrs. Farleigh, you're not serious, are you?"

“Mr. Griebel, I am serious.” Stone faced, former Congresswoman May Farleigh began her tale. “It all started twenty eight years ago. My boyfriend and I were living together in a small apartment in the city. I was only twenty-four at the time. I was young and impressionable, and shocked by the poverty and violence of the city. To see so much suffering after a childhood of suburban ignorance filled me with grief for the less fortunate and guilt for the blessings that my birthright had bestowed upon me.

“For months I traversed the city in a daze, dwelling depressingly on thoughts of poverty, sprawl and the death of the American spirit. I walked the avenues in a daydream, trying to make sense of the suffering around me. Then one day while waiting for a bus by Bodhi’s Department store, it all came together.

“I was leaning against a lamppost, envisioning the poor, protesting masses dressed all in blacks and greys, chanting at an iron gate, shouting for dignity, when a powerful darkness overcame me. I felt dizzy and fell to my knees.

"When I stood up, everything was clear. I had been dwelling too long on poverty, discrimination and the muted spirit of the city and how they came to be, rather than how they might be eliminated. In that instant, my thoughts turned inside out. I saw cause and effect as two ends of the same rope. The interconnectedness of all things revealed itself. To end society's suffering; all we had to do was start down the path of healing. That was the day I decided to enter politics.

"At first, my boyfriend teased me. *May, you won't change the world. You're such a dreamer.* But when he realized how determined I was, he got behind me. I wasn't sure how I was going to do it; I just knew that I *was* going to do it. Then one day a friend mentioned that she was going to a fundraiser after work for the local councilman, Tom Peters. I met Tom that night. My friend just dragged me right up to him and introduced us. It should have been obvious, but wouldn't you know how gracious he was, and charming. We chatted over little plates of cheese and grapes. I told him about my ideas and poured my heart out to him. I told him that I wanted to get involved in politics.

"From then on, the door was open to me. Tom became my mentor. That fall, I worked the phones for his campaign, and planted lawn signs around town. Tom won by a landslide, and after he won, he helped me get a job at city hall. The next year I ran for the Board of Education, and with Tom's help and connections, I was easily elected. One year later, Tom ran for Congress, and I ran for his seat on the council. We both won, but tragically he died of a heart attack soon after swearing in. In the wake of the tragedy, the powers-that-be backed me in the special election, and I spent the next twenty four years serving in the United States Congress."

May paused to take a breath. There was a slight slouch in her shoulders and a look of defeat across her face. Otto quickly stepped in. "Mrs. Farleigh, that's an amazing story. Of course it's unfortunate that your mentor passed away so soon, but your rapid rise to power is stunning. Surely those must have been exciting times?"

May frowned. "Exciting, yes. In the beginning, I was very excited. I was fired up. I wasn't even thirty years old and already I was someone. My boyfriend and I got married before we moved to Washington. We both felt the world at our fingertips and I was ready to build the world according to my vision. But it wasn't long before my bubble burst. Not only did no one else share my vision, no one wanted to hear about it. I was young and female. The party leaders sidelined me on pointless subcommittees and never backed my bills. They were more interested in serving their campaign contributors than fighting for values like equality or sustainability. Before I knew it, I hadn't accomplished anything but it was already time to campaign again, and I was pregnant with my daughter. My husband and I were just getting used to the Washington life. We figured we might as well keep it up.

"In my first re-election campaign I stayed true to my ideology, but I ran an aggressive campaign. No door went unknocked and no lamppost unleafleted. As the years went by my campaigns grew uglier and uglier, full of attack ads and slander. Eventually I was re-elected to Congress eleven times.

"In the early days, with my pretty face and youngish looks, I was a media darling. I was in front of a camera or microphone sometimes eight hours a day. The pomp and prestige of politics overcame me. I spent my days sitting in committee meetings and my nights socializing at galas and balls, hobnobbing with the hoity-toity. Sure, without a passion for change, the working days became boring. How long can one person listen to so many problems and do nothing about it? How many times can you shake a voter's hand and pretend that you care? But it was a small sacrifice for power. Plus the money was good, so election after election I fought more and more viciously for my seat. Then not long after my fiftieth birthday, I had an accident. I drank too much wine at a fundraiser and crashed my car on the way home.

What made it worse was the involvement of a male companion in the passenger seat, who was injured in the accident, but wasn't my husband."

May paused and took a breath. She looked sullen. "Nothing gets ratings like a celebrity smear campaign. The media turned on me quickly. *The Drunken Floosy* they called me. I spent the next eight weeks with a cast on my leg, lying in bed hearing my name all over the evening news. I dove into the bottle of pain meds prescribed by my doctor and I reached a real low. I looked back on my life and realized how hopeful and optimistic I once was, and how cynical and self-serving I'd become. I was ashamed of myself. I contemplated suicide."

May stopped talking. There was quiet in the courtroom. The sound of the parrot preening himself could be heard above a quiet murmur. Ruth in the jury box was shaking her head judgingly. The survivalists chewed their fingernails, while the Buddhists meditated on the idea of interconnectedness. The twins were thumb wrestling.

Their tongues hung droolingly from their mouths. Otto addressed the Congresswoman. "Mrs. Farleigh, what happened next?"

"Much like my awakening many years ago, I was soaking in the tub when my ears popped and I became instantly aware. Politics had ruined my life. After more than two decades I had forgotten why I decided to enter politics in the first place. I was no longer involved to make a difference. I was simply addicted to the drama. I was hooked on the status. But in the fog, I missed out on the rest of my life. I had spent my days at boring hearings while I could have been taking care of my daughter. I spent too many nights fundraising with special interests and corporate donors, while I could have been home cooking dinner. I weekended with the well connected, when I could have picnicked with my family. My marriage was in tatters and my daughter wouldn't speak to me. All those years of fundraisers and finger foods had left me fat. In that tub I suddenly realized politics had ruined my life. Half a lifetime ago I set off to help others. In the process, not only did I let down my constituents; I hurt my loved ones and myself too.

"But who's to blame? The politicians? The donors? The media? Voters? Nonvoters? Yes, yes, yes, yes and yes. Everyone is to blame. Everyone is responsible for the mechanisms of our democracy, and the people we place at the helm. The state of politics is our own doing. It was my undoing. Its failure will be everyone else's undoing, and it's everyone's fault."

Otto interrupted May for one last question. "Mrs. Farleigh, after all that has transpired, how would you say your life is going today?" May's smile returned to her face. She perked up and addressed Otto. "Today I'm doing well. My family and I are reconciling. Sure, I'll always be a recovering politician, but I haven't touched a newspaper in months and this Fall I'll be enrolling in culinary school. I'm going to be a chef. And I'm going to spend more time with my family."

"Mrs. Farleigh, thank you very much." Otto clasped his hands and then looked at the jury and Judge Bacchus. *Six up, six down,* he thought to himself. Everyone hit his or her key points. As the Plaintiffs had testified, corporations, politicians, the media, and voters – everyone in one way or another – was guilty for the state of society. He hoped the jury saw it the same way. "No further questions, Your Honor." Otto declared.

The Public Defender penciled in the last empty box of his crossword puzzle. He had no questions. With no one else to testify, Otto Griebel addressed Judge Bacchus and proudly declared, "The Plaintiff rests its case, Your Honor."

XIII

The Illuminati

Having solved the final corner of his crossword puzzle, with 69-Across, "*A victim*", the Public Defender filled in the last answer, 'MARK', thus placing the 'R' in 52-Down, "*One of the Seven Sins*", 'GREED'. It was now the Public Defender's turn to call a witness. So the Public Defender stood up from his table, and shuffled to the center of the room. His fly was unzipped.

"Ladies and gentlemen of the Jury, the Plaintiff alleges that the sordid state of society is somehow everyone's fault. They have laid blame on corporations, politicians, the media, voters and everyone else. Well frankly, I don't get it. I don't have any witnesses either. But I do have this!"

The Public Defender pulled a black cassette out of his baggy jacket pocket. "I submit this video as evidence that everyone is not guilty." Judge Bacchus asked, "What is this evidence that you are submitting?"

The Public Defender answered, "This is a video that came to me in the mail just yesterday, which will clearly show that everyone is not guilty."

Judge Bacchus looked questioningly at Otto. Confident in his case, Otto simply shrugged his shoulders. Judge Bacchus replied to the Public Defender. "Your evidence may be presented." Then turning to Bailiff Anton Brown, "Would the Bailiff please bring the television set."

Anton Brown opened a closet in the wood paneling behind the media booth and slipped out of view. There was knocking, and banging, and then the sound of something crashing followed by muffled cursing. A moment later, Anton Brown rolled out a 27" TV on a wheeled stand with a VCR. He rolled it through the doorway into place in front of the witness stand. He picked up an extension cord from a shelf on the stand and plugged in the set to an outlet just behind the American flag. The VCR clunked to life and sucked in the tape. The audience murmured, as the image of two well-known men in leather armchairs appeared on the screen.

Billionaire tycoon Donald Trump and former President George W. Bush sat stoically in red leather chairs in a carpeted room surrounded by walls of books. A fire crackled in the fireplace. The video had been made several days earlier; put together by a group of Illuminati intent on preventing this case from making a bigger mess out of society than it already was. They knew exactly what the Plaintiff would say, as they had bugged Otto's office and were well aware of everyone's grievances.

Donald Trump, dressed in a dark grey suit, blew his floppy orange hair out of his eyes and spoke to the camera. "Good citizens of America, President Bush and I have been sent here to demonstrate why everyone is NOT guilty. Everyone loves to blame CEO's and corporations for the oppression of the workingman. Good citizens lament how executives command soaring salaries while the average man muddles about for minimum wage, and how executives' bonuses double after mass layoffs.

"Firstly, if it weren't for the threat of layoffs, the workingman wouldn't work as hard as he does. If the workingman didn't work as hard as he does, Pepsi would cost double. No one would afford a car and everyone would be living in his or her parents' basement. So be grateful. Without layoffs, the economy would be as weak as the Greeks'.

"Secondly, CEO's are people too. Workers complain that their bosses make too much, but the brave men and women who lead our nation's greatest firms have peers to impress too. Yachts, villas and

Rolex watches are necessities in the world of the rich and famous.

"So don't be bothered by executive bonuses and corporate stock options. They'd be a victimless crime if they weren't legal. Printing company stock and buying it at a discount is no different than the Federal Reserve placing imaginary zeros at the end of big banks' balance sheets. You can't feel it in your wallet, and you shouldn't feel it in your heart. Besides, if you were in the CEO's shoes, you would take the stock options too. So you can't blame CEO's, and since you can't blame them, they can't be guilty. If CEO's aren't guilty, then surely everyone isn't guilty."

Donald Trump picked up a snifter of whiskey from a small table next to his chair. He swirled the amber liquor around the cup and took a sip. He looked at President Bush who took the queue.

"Fellow Americans, as a former President with nothing to lose, it is incumbent upon me to tell you why everyone isn't guilty. Ask yourselves this. At the last election, did you really have a choice? Or were most of your candidates at the local, state and federal level, running un-opposed or against a candidate with a drug problem, criminal record, or history of tax evasion? How many of the candidates on the ballot were egotists, out of touch, or beholden more to their donors than to basic values like honesty and compassion? Under those circumstances, you can't blame voters for choosing crummy politicians because their only choices *are* crummy politicians.

"Then ask yourselves this. What issues really get you going? As a voter, do you get excited about things like infrastructure or the environment? Or are you more worked up by gun control and taxes? You can't blame politicians for pandering. It's the only way to get elected. As soon as politicians explain how they'll fix the economy, everyone finds some reason to disagree with their plan. But when politicians just say they *will* fix the economy, everyone agrees it's the right thing to do. Just as the armadillo hides behind its armor, politicians hide behind vague promises. It's a survival instinct.

"So you see, you can't blame politicians for pandering, and you can't blame voters for electing crummy politicians. If the voters and the politicians can't be blamed, then they can't be guilty. Since they're not guilty, everyone isn't guilty. Good luck and may God bless the United States of America."

President Bush crossed his legs and leaned back in his chair. Donald Trump stood up and walked towards the camera. His gray-twilled crotch loomed large for a moment. The image shook and went blank.

The Public Defender returned to the center of the room and addressed Judge Bacchus. "I rest my case, Your Honor." Judge Bacchus looked at Otto. Otto shrugged again. Without a witness to cross-examine there was nothing more he could do. Then Judge Bacchus spoke. "Ladies and gentlemen of the court, we will have a short recess, followed by closing arguments, at which point the jury will retire for deliberations."

XIV

Third Recess

During the recess, the room was abuzz with chatter. The Bombshells were busy arguing with the one-eyed man. It was a clear-cut case. The jury would find everyone guilty, the Bombshells argued. The Plaintiff's case was too solid. "No", said the one-eyed man. "The videotape introduced enough logical doubt. It's all too simple. When was the last time someone who wasn't blamed, was ever found guilty? Never. Therefore, if you can't blame CEO's, politicians or voters for the state of society, then you can't blame everyone. And if you can't blame everyone, everyone isn't guilty."

“Ah”, the Bombshells argued, “but you’re hung up on the idea of logical doubt. But what use is logical doubt in a court of law, if it isn’t reasonable? Only with reasonable doubt can the jury acquit the Defendant, and the Defense’s argument certainly isn’t reasonable. How can it be reasonable that so few should profit while so many are falling behind or staying behind. How can it be reasonable when our health and arts are compromised by the profit motive? If none of that is reasonable then there’s no reasonable doubt that everyone is guilty. Everyone must be guilty, because everyone *is* guilty.” The one-eyed man wasn’t convinced. The parrot on his shoulder preened himself and repeated the word *guilty* in a quiet squawk.

Across the aisle Arthur stewed. He peered off dejectedly into the jury box. *Dammit,* he thought. *The guys at work are going to tear me apart if this thing falls through. And that jury does not look convinced.* May was starting to think she didn’t sell her case enough. Gus realized how much more he had to say. He wished he could get back up there and tell everyone what he really thought. Jackie Lim just wanted to get this thing over with. If it ended early, she might make it to the gym before it closed. Greta was anxious to see her dog Charlie, and maybe have something to eat.

In the jury box, Ruth vigorously scribbled on a pad of paper, flipping the pages quickly as she scrawled with a ballpoint pen. The Buddhist monks were deep in thought, meditating with their hands folded neatly inside their maroon robes. Their foreheads were smooth and calm like a mountain lake on a windless day. They contemplated the origin of suffering and whether everyone was responsible for everyone's suffering or if something else were afoot. More importantly, would a large transfer of money be the right means to end everyone's suffering? Their minds were not made up. Next to them, one of the survivalists had invited the Siamese twins to sit on his lap while his two friends dismantled the twins' chair into, wood, brackets and bolts. The survivalists were preparing to fashion shivs to aid their escape. Finally, Judge Bacchus called the court back to order.

"Ladies and gentlemen," Judge Bacchus spoke, "we will now continue with the proceedings. Attorney Griebel will make his closing arguments first. Mr. Griebel, please take the floor."

XV

Closing Remarks

Otto buttoned his dark navy suit jacket. He placed his palms on the oak table before him and stood up. After the day's long proceedings, his perfectly parted hair looked as good as it did at the start. There wasn't a wrinkle in his suit. Confidently, Otto stepped to the center of the courtroom and the world's attention. The Bombshells in the front row swooned as Otto addressed the jury.

"Ladies and gentlemen of the jury, the case before you is clear. Society is what everyone makes it. Everyone is responsible for the world we live in, and the world we live in is causing everyone harm. Therefore everyone is guilty and restitution is due.

"Look inside yourself. Inside of everyone, is a little bit of Arthur Jay, Tyrone Jenkins and Greta Gernhart. Who isn't trying to get ahead? Who doesn't feel that they're stuck in neutral? Who doesn't feel the safety net growing thinner every year?

"Who doesn't mourn the death of popular culture or dream big like Jackie Lim? Who doesn't care for the Earth and the animals, at least just a little, like Doctor Jeremiah? Who hasn't tried to change the world like Congresswoman Farleigh, or had their heart broken in the process?

"Ladies and gentlemen of the jury, if you can feel the pain of the six Plaintiffs who have testified today, then you can feel the pain in your heart too. As these six have been wronged, so too have you been wronged. The evidence is clear.

"In the land of the free, corporations have enslaved the working man, chaining him to his desk in exchange for a mortgage and a car, while those of lesser birthright are thrown into private prisons, where every prisoner is just another penny for some rich man's pocket. In the same spirit of profit, our doctors and pharmacies bankrupt the elderly, and no one stands in their way.

"Meanwhile, the vested interests scuttle our airwaves with the static of cheap talk radio and artificially preserved pop music. Our newscasts grow more vapid by the day. In an age of limitless information we're force fed celebrity gossip and tomorrow's weather.

"While these offences go unpunished, the few at the top solidify their titles and entitlements, through boards, trusts, and cozy political relations. Not even the environment is safe from the profit motive. In the home of the brave, the courts treat corporations like people, and politicians are a brand. When our basic values are for sale, and the scales of justice appear cast against the cliffs of apathy, there's nothing left to do but give up and go home."

Otto paused. He looked Ruth in the eye. "But I won't go home. The Plaintiffs in the class action lawsuit of Everyone versus Everyone won't let me go home without a fight. So I say to you, you must find in favor of the Plaintiff. The evidence and logic are indisputable. Society has wronged everyone in one way or another, and everyone is responsible. Even inaction is action. Whether we actively participate, or just sit on the sidelines, the results are all our doing."

Then Otto turned to the audience, caught eyes with the one-eyed man and the parrot on his shoulder and yelled with bravado, "That is why you must find the Defendant…Guilty!"

The parrot squawked. Otto turned back to Ruth and the jury. "Thank you for your time today." Then he bowed to Judge Bacchus. "I rest my case, Your Honor."

Otto slid back into his seat at the Plaintiff's table and unbuttoned his suit jacket. In the back of the audience, the shirtless Texan let out a little *yeehaw* and the Caribbean man beat a quick *ratatatata* on his drum. Judge Bacchus knocked his gavel to quiet the room. "Public Defender, your closing remarks please."

The Public Defender stood up and walked to the center of the room. The television cameras all zoomed in on what appeared to be toilet paper stuck to his shoe. He was undeterred.

"Ladies and gentlemen of the jury. Thank you for your participation in this trial, but the truth is that this trial was a farce. The Plaintiff would have you believe that everyone is responsible for the state of society, and therefore guilty for the harm society has caused us. Well I don't get it. So let me finally ask a few questions of my own." The Public Defender stuck his thumbs in his waistline and puffed out his chest, stressing the buttons of his shirt.

"When you get into your car in the morning, and drive to work, who is in your way? When you're in line at the store, and someone before you is paying in change, writing a check, or talking on their cell phone, who is wasting your time? When you are annoyed with the world, who drives you crazy? Is it everyone? Or is it everyone else? It's everyone else of course. Which means everyone else is guilty but me, which is probably also how you see it, which means that collectively, everyone is guilty."

The Public Defender stopped to think about what he just said. Confused somewhat, he continued.

"Ladies and gentlemen of the jury, the evidence and testimony presented to you today is irrelevant. Contrary to Attorney Griebel's claim, there's no logic in it. Everyone can't be guilty if everyone else is, and besides, you can't blame them. In any other man's shoes, we'd all do the same. You can't blame anyone, and if you can't blame anyone, then you can't blame everyone. If you can't blame everyone, then everyone isn't guilty.

"As they say in Greek, Q.E.D. quod erat demonstrandum. Case closed."

The Public Defender turned to Judge Bacchus, clapped his hands in conclusion and said with the satisfaction of a job well done, "I rest my case, Your Honor." The Public Defender returned to his seat and noticed the toilet paper on the bottom of his shoe. Judge Bacchus swung his gavel. "Ladies and gentlemen, we will now adjourn for jury deliberation." Then addressing the jurors, "Jurors, you've heard the arguments today. Now, without bias or prejudice, the court requires that you weigh the arguments before you. If you find that everyone has caused everyone harm, then you must find everyone guilty." Then addressing Anton Brown, he said, "Bailiff, please lead the jury to their chamber."

XVI

Jury Deliberations

Bailiff Anton Brown walked across the courtroom to the jury box. He passed stenographer Mary-Jane Reefer, who rolled back from her desk, revealing her long slender legs. Anton Brown looked down at her and smiled. Ruth grimaced at the two of them. *Enough of this hanky-panky,* she thought. Anton Brown swung open the gate to the jury box and Ruth stood up. The sudden movement awakened the bald headed monks from their meditation. They opened their eyes as the bearded survivalists stood up, yawning and stretching their arms. Sensing something afoot, the twins began to mumble agitatedly. Their ponytails swayed back and forth as they bobbled their heads with confusion.

"Come with me," the bailiff said. He held open the swinging gate and let the group of eight out. In single file, Ruth led the robed monks, the scraggly bearded survivalists and the googly-eyed twins to their chambers where they lunched earlier in the day. Anton Brown walked behind them shaking his head. *This is the stupidest thing I've ever been a part* of, he thought. *But damn if I couldn't use the money.* When the jury settled into their chamber, Anton addressed them. "Okay, folks. Take your time. You've heard the arguments. You've heard Judge Bacchus's instructions. When you're ready, Miss Ruth, as juror number one, we ask that you prepare to read the verdict. If you need water or food or have any questions, knock twice. When you've reached your conclusion knock three times. Now I'll be locking the door so that no one can disturb you."

Anton Brown exited the chamber. The door latch clicked. The jury was now sitting alone at a round table. No one said a word. The monks were still. The survivalists were sharpening their shivs with brackets from the twins' disassembled chair. One way or another, they were going back home today. The twins were picking each other's ears.

Sensing her responsibility, Ruth addressed her fellow jurors. "Who here thinks everyone is guilty?" No one said a word. The twins blinked. "OK then," Ruth said. "How about you two?" she asked, looking at the monks. The Monks stared back quietly.

All trial long, the monks had mediated long and hard on the case presented before them. They examined the evidence before them and framed it within the Four Noble Truths, the tenets of their faith. Number one, suffering exists. Number two, suffering has its cause. Number three, healing can come to be, and number four, there is a path toward healing.

The monks first asked themselves, *was everyone suffering?* The answer was obvious, *of course.* Through the course of their meditation, they then asked, *is it everyone's fault that everyone is suffering?* Again, the answer was obvious. *Yes, everyone is suffering because of the actions, inaction and expectations of everyone, everyone else, and themself.* Guilt was obvious, but guilt alone was not enough for the two Buddhists. This case wasn't just about guilt, but about restitution.

Continuing with their meditation, the monks asked, *if everyone is the cause of everyone's suffering, is the end of suffering possible?* Again, the answer was crystal clear. The end of suffering is always possible. The real question is *how.* Throughout the proceedings, the monks struggled mostly with the fourth question. *Will sixteen trillion dollars provide a pathway to end everyone's suffering?* Back and forth their thoughts flowed like tides in a stormy ocean until after a long day of right attention and right thought they reached the obvious conclusion. *Hell yes. Sixteen trillion dollars WOULD make a difference.* The real problem was how they would get a piece of the pie this late in the game. But as fate would have it, the monks had taken a vow of silence and were unable to answer Ruth's question.

Realizing that the monks were of no help, and seeing the twins picking each other's nose, Ruth tried the survivalists. "How about you three, now? How do you feel about this whole big travesty that we've witnessed?" Survivalist number one answered for his buddies, whose pockets were now filled with shivs and several bottles of water from a table at the back of the room. "Ma'am, it's up to you. As soon as we see our chance, we're sneaking out of here and heading right back to camp."

Ruth frowned. She was on her own. She flipped through her notes from the day and prayed. *Lord, I spent many long months in a coma. I survived thanks to your grace, and now you've brought me here to decide man's fate. I don't understand your ways, but I believe in them.* Ruth felt the Holy Spirit come into her body and she began to scribble.

The jury has been asked to determine if everyone is guilty of causing harm to everyone through negligence or direct action.

Everyone is guilty of negligence – negligence towards God, God's word and God's mission. Arthur Jay and Tyrone Jenkins, guilty of greed, guilty for failing to appreciate what they have. If the grass is always greener somewhere, it's also browner somewhere else. Even Mr. Jenkins, guilty of thievery, is as guilty as Arthur Jay for not appreciating the shelter over his head or the food in his belly. Mr. Gus, guilty of preaching death against those who disagree with him, rather than using love to educate the world to his mission. Mrs. Farleigh and Miss Lim, guilty of vanity, guilty of seeking fame and attention rather than humble service to the Lord, guilty of making idols of themselves. Mrs. Gernhart, guilty for failing to help herself. She would rather curse the doctors who tried to heal her than thank them for their effort. I didn't spend a lifetime working hard, raising my children, and worshipping the Lord's good word to let people make a mockery of society.

Everyone is too quick to place blame on others, rather than find guilt within. Though everyone is guilty, it is not for the reasons argued today, and therefore the jury finds the Defendant, not guilty.

Ruth put her pen down and reread her statement. Then she underlined *not guilty.* Ruth didn't know what else to say. She sat quietly chewing on her pen. *I guess that's it,* she thought. She looked at her fellow jurors. "If no one has anything to say, then let's get on with it." Ruth got up from the table and went to the door. *Knockknockknock.* She knocked three times. The latch clicked, and the door opened. Anton Brown poked his head through the crack and asked, "Already?" Ruth nodded. Anton shrugged. "Alright then. I'll tell the Judge and come back for you in two minutes."

Two minutes later, Anton Brown returned to lead the jury back to the courtroom. Otto, the Plaintiffs, the Public Defender and the public were already in their seats in the courtroom. The red lights of the media's big black cameras blinked back to life. Everyone around the world was watching live on television. No one was breathing. The world's stomach was in a knot, waiting to hear what Ruth would say. Judge Bacchus swung his gavel. The knock echoed across the room and the airwaves. "Will the jury please read their verdict?"

XVII

The Verdict

Ruth stood up from her seat at the corner of the jury box. She looked regal. Her beautiful dark skin radiated behind her royal purple robe. A well-placed light shone a halo above her head. She held her notes on a small piece of yellow paper in her hands. She cleared her throat and unfolded her remarks. She had spent many long months in a coma and she wasn't going to spend two more minutes in this courtroom. She looked down at her notes. Then she folded them in half and addressed the court. She felt God's presence in the room. A feeling of euphoria crept up her spine. Ruth spoke from the heart in her rich, deep Jamaican accent. "We, the jurors, were asked to determine if everyone has caused everyone some amount of suffering, and whether restitution is due. After deliberation with each other and the good Lord above, we the jury find the Defendant..."

"Guilty!" squawked the parrot from the top of the one-eyed man's shoulder. Before Ruth could say another word, Judge Bacchus swung his gavel. "Case closed!" he shouted. He pressed a big red button under his desk. Red, white and blue confetti dropped from the ceiling. Stenographer Mary-Jane Reefer uncorked a bottle of bubbling Champaign and leapt into the arms of Bailiff Anton Brown. The Bombshells squealed with delight. They would have their furs after all! The audience high-fived and hugged. The Caribbean man started up his drumming again. *Ratatata rata tat. Ratatata rata tat.* Car horns and fireworks could be heard from outside the courtroom. Tyrone began to pump his fists back and forth. He leaned back and yelled as if he just won the Super Bowl. Greta sobbed on Jackie's shoulder, finally releasing all of the stress and emotion that had been building in the weeks leading up to the trial. Arthur Jay was numb. *Does this mean I'm guilty,* he asked himself. He thought victory would feel liberating, but all he felt was the urge for a stiff drink. The story of Doctor Frankenstein came to Arthur's mind as red confetti settled on his head and shoulders.

In the media box, CBS and Al Jazeera lit up cigars. The local reporter pulled a flask out of his vest. Fox News dipped Miss Telemundo and kissed her. Miss Telemundo slapped Fox News, sending him tumbling into CNN, which sent everyone and their cameras spilling to the floor. While the live feed was down in the courtroom, the survivalists slinked away, escaping with their shivs and a dozen bottles of water, headed home to Yellowstone.

And so it went. Society absolutely lost its mind for the next forty-eight hours. Cities were looted. Shop windows were smashed. Police cars were flipped over and set on fire. People were so excited that they didn't know what to do but riot. Since everyone but Ruth was celebrating, there were no policemen or army to quell the chaos. Thousands died in the immediate aftermath from widespread mayhem and irrational exuberance. Eventually, the President asked Judge Bacchus to address the nation in order to calm the crowds.

After two days of terror, Judge Bacchus took to the airwaves, dressed in a Hawaiian shirt. He sipped wine from a bottle, while palm trees swayed behind him in a gentle breeze. In a calm tone and slurred speech, Judge Bacchus explained the next steps. Within two weeks he would determine the terms of the settlement and checks would be issued. He appealed to the public for peace and asked that firemen go back to work. His announcement was enough to distract the masses for an evening and put a halt to the chaos. Firemen did go back to work. A nervous peace settled over the masses.

Two weeks later, Judge Bacchus took to the airwaves one last time to explain where the money would come from and how much money everyone would receive. In the same Hawaiian shirt, with his long wavy gray hair tied neatly in the back, Judge Maxwell Bacchus explained to the American people and the world how the case of Everyone versus Everyone would be settled. Sixteen trillion dollars was a lot of money to find and divvy up after all.

As explained by Judge Bacchus, everyone had been wronged to greater or lesser degrees. After much drinking, and much deliberation, Judge Bacchus settled on a sliding scale that operated on broad based terms that everyone would understand. It was settled that all citizens of voting age would receive a varying amount. The young and healthy were to receive the most as they were likely to live longer and would need more money than those with one foot in the grave. Judge Bacchus also considered gender bias. Women, having been underpaid for generations, would receive twenty percent more than men. Along similar lines of racial logic, white people would receive the least, followed in order by Asians, Latinos and the Black community. Black people, having been most disadvantaged by society would need the most to overcome the imbalance. Then all of that was adjusted through a complex calculation to adjust for factors like income, recorded vocabulary at the first grade and parents' education so that those who were the most disadvantaged would receive more. Immigrants received a pro-rated amount based on their years as a citizen, with illegal aliens receiving a sufficient sum to afford a first class ticket back to their home country. Within all of that calculating, nothing was set-aside for the Native Americans. Judge Bacchus had completely forgotten about them. All in all, the average check totaled $65,000.

Then Judge Bacchus explained where the money would come from. First, the entire national park system and all their mineral rights were sold to China for half the total. Before the year was over, the Chinese would build the world's largest geo-thermal trinket factory, smack dab where Old Faithful had faithfully sprayed every hour on the hour for as long as man remembered. The survivalists watched in horror from a green grassy knoll as an official raised the blood red Chinese flag during the groundbreaking ceremony.

The remainder of the money came in smaller chunks. The bank accounts of the wealthy were emptied to the point that they were no richer than anyone else after the repayment. While that should have yielded as much as ten trillion dollars, only a fraction was recovered. The wealthy had wisely hidden most of their assets in anticipation of the verdict. To compensate, the national sports leagues were put in hock to the generous Saudi royal family for a cool trillion. Change came quickly to the big leagues. Baseballers made the crescent sign instead of the cross. Footballers stopped thanking Jesus in interviews, and offered praise instead to Allah. The ladies of the Women's National Basketball Association were made to play in burkas, which really disrupted the passing game. To cover the remaining five trillion, the Federal Reserve produced an equal dollar share of $200 and $500 bills with the likenesses of Barack Obama and Ronald Reagan. Pennies, nickels and dimes became worthless overnight.

Ten days later, the checks came in the mail. Check cashing firms and liquor stores made a racket in the cities. Around the country, there were major shortages of cars and electronics. Small riots flared up at big box stores in every state, where angry shoppers argued over the last of the big screen televisions. Hundreds were shanked in the first hours alone. The stock market went wild with volatility. Within a few short weeks, inflation was through the roof. The dollar plummeted against other major currencies. The price of milk and petrol tripled.

Sure, everyone won, but hardly anyone was better off. Arthur Jay finally had money but still couldn't get a contractor on the phone. Greta paid off her medical bills and went right back to zero. Gus's disgust for society was only reinforced by the people's post verdict behavior. Fed up, he decided to protect the elephants himself or die trying. He spent his windfall on the last rifle on Wal-Mart's shelf and a one-way ticket to Kenya.

On the other hand, Jackie Lim spent her check on music equipment and a personal trainer. Within six months she had a record deal. Former Congresswoman May Farleigh finished culinary school and reconciled with her husband and daughter. To help the healing process, they opened a food truck together. The falling dollar made fuel so expensive that they were forced to sell tacos out of their driveway. But business was gangbusters!

And what about Tyrone Jenkins? As soon as his check cleared, Tyrone hopped on a flight to Las Vegas with a briefcase full of cash, walked straight up to the roulette table at the Palms Casino and placed the gutsiest bet you ever saw. "Go big or go home!" he yelled, fists pumping, as the little white ball bounced around the spinning wheel. His bright eyes watched with ecstasy as the tiny ball settled on lucky 18 at 35:1 odds. After the wildest night of his life, Tyrone Jenkins flew home in a private jet and bought his mama a house on the spot.

As it went, Tyrone did well. Some landlords and business owners also made a tidy sum during the initial spending spree. But no one made out better than Attorney Otto Griebel. After taking a thirty percent cut for his lawyer fees, Otto was the richest man in the world.

The End

About the Author

Arthur Jay is an American writer and engineer. His first book, Fraternity House, was self-published in print and e-book, June 2014. Visit www.arthurjay.com for up to date news and info.

About the Artist

Cover art and design by Dave Estes.

Visit www.dave-estes.com for news and info.

Made in United States
North Haven, CT
04 November 2026

21771560R00088